PSYCHOLOGY VERSUS BIBLICAL COUNSELING

Does the Church Need Psychology?

According as his divine power hath given unto us all things that *pertain* unto life and godliness, through the knowledge of him that hath called us to glory and virtue... *— 2 Peter 1:3*

PSYCHOLOGY VERSUS BIBLICAL COUNSELING

Does the Church Need Psychology?

By

Romeo B. Macale, PhD, EdD, ThD, DMin, DD

iv

ISBN: 9781728934129

First Paperback Edition, October 2018

All Scripture quotations are taken from the King James Version of 1611 unless otherwise indicated. The reference-system adopted throughout this book is the so-called: *Harvard-Footnote Reference System*.

KJV 1611 Press
Perth, WA, Australia
www.mbbc.com.au

Printed in the United States of America

DEDICATION

This book
is dedicated to my longsuffering,
sacrificial, kind, loving, beautiful, intelligent,
educated, sweet and wonderful Christian wife, Ethel
Macale, and my lovely, kind, respectful, beautiful,
intelligent, educated, and wonderful Christian
daughter, Thelmoore Ruth Macale. Primarily, this
work is humbly dedicated most especially to my One
and Only Saviour – the Lord Jesus Christ.

For the word of God *is* quick, and powerful, and sharper than any twoedged sword, piercing even to the dividing asunder of soul and spirit, and of the joints and marrow, and *is* a discerner of the thoughts and intents of the heart.

— Hebrews 4:12

PREFACE

This book discusses the subject: ***The Superiority of biblical counselling over psychological counselling***. Particularly, it tries to argue that psychological counselling is an inferior treatment therapy to the problems of living. It places its stamp on biblical counselling as the key and proper solution for problems of human behaviour. It defines and explains counselling form the viewpoint of the Scriptures. The Bible presents superior instruction, expertise, authority, cure, evidence, and product in dealing with problems of living.

Biblical counselling has a superior instruction in the sense that the Bible demands absolute obedience for one to have a lasting cure. It has a superior expertise because the Bible has been written by God – the author of man. It is only the Bible that has the authority to prescribe solution for problems of living since it is inspired by God. The long lasting cure cannot be found anywhere but in the Bible. The overwhelming evidence of cured and transformed lives is due to God's power through His Word. It God's Word has the power to transform people, it is but a foregone conclusion that its product are quality ones.

Finally, my brethren, be strong in the Lord, and in the power of his might. Put on the whole armour of God, that ye may be able to stand against the wiles of the devil. For we wrestle not against flesh and blood, but against principalities, against powers, against the rulers of the darkness of this world, against spiritual wickedness in high *places*. Wherefore take unto you the whole armour of God, that ye may be able to withstand in the evil day, and having done all, to stand. Stand therefore, having your loins girt about with truth, and having on the breastplate of righteousness; And your feet shod with the preparation of the gospel of peace; Above all, taking the shield of faith, wherewith ye shall be able to quench all the fiery darts of the wicked. And take the helmet of salvation, and the sword of the Spirit, which is the word of God: Praying always with all prayer and supplication in the Spirit, and watching thereunto with all perseverance — and supplication for all saints; — *Ephesians 6:10-18*

TABLE OF CONTENTS

Call unto me, and I will answer thee, and shew thee great and mighty things, which thou knowest not. *– Jeremiah 33:3*

CHAPTER 1

Introduction

Before discussing the issue on *The Superiority of Biblical Counseling over Psychological Counseling*, it is but necessary to clarify and define some terms or phrases as used in this paper. **Counseling** refers to advices or therapies believed to be cures for problems of living that are administered by pastors, Christians, professional or non-professional counselors. The term **biblical counseling** uses the Bible as the only standard for counseling people suffering from problems of living. While **psychological counseling** uses the opinions of men, unproven and unscientific theories and techniques of unredeemed men and women. The phrase **problems of living** refers to inorganic diseases such as alcoholism, drug addiction, and the like. **Mental illness, mental disease, mental disorder,** and **dysfunction** refer to all kinds of problems of living (Bobgan 1987, p. 133).

Psychologists, psychiatrists, mental health professionals, and other men who are against the Scriptures have always derided that *mental diseases* are beyond the jurisdiction of biblical counselors such as pastors, preachers, or faithful Christians. They allege the latter have no technical skills, qualifications, and authority to deal with mental diseases. Psychologists (Bobgan 1987, p. 8), however, do admit biblical counselors can deal with problems of living but *not* mental diseases. And lots of other reasoning that can be found in this paper allegedly demonstrating that biblical counseling is outside the bounds of problems of living.

Reasons for the Superiority
of Biblical Counseling

The issue to be resolved in the case at bar is: ***Whether or not biblical counseling is superior over psychological counseling.*** That, biblical counseling is superior over psychological counseling is beyond doubt. There are six compelling reasons to sustain this contention, to wit: instruction, expertise, authority, cure, evidence, and product.

Superior Bible-based Instruction

Firstly, that, biblical counseling has a superior Bible-based instruction. This instruction is only found in the Bible, which is the basis of biblical counseling. The *first* instruction to man is obedience to God. He demands absolute obedience from man (1 Samuel 15:22; Deuteronomy 30:16-18). It is obedience to God that determines well-being, success, or joy. It is disobedience to God that produces sin, sickness, problems of living, and other miseries. The classic example of this is when the first man Adam decided to disobey God of His one and only instruction not to eat the forbidden fruit (Genesis 2:16-17). The Bible records Adam utterly violated this direct and simple instruction (Genesis 3). As a consequence he sinned

4

against God. Adam's sin causes all sorts of problems of living, medical diseases, environmental degradation and destruction.

Psychological counseling has tried to improve this human malady by following the instruction of men's opinions and rejects Bible teaching. *One*, it rejects the biblical teaching that sin causes all sorts of "mental disorders." Psychology supplanted this biblical instruction with the opinions of unredeemed men (Counseling Methods Survey) such as Freud, Jung, Rogers, Adler, Maslow, Fromm, Watson, Skinner, and lots of others. Freud (Bobgan, The Psychoanalytic Stream…) castigated God, the Bible, and religion as causes of mental problems. To reject God and espouse his Psychoanalysis Theory is the antidote for mental disorders.

However, Freud's psychoanalysis never solves problems of living. His ideas no matter how brilliant in human terms are under God's judgment. Psychoanalysis is full of flaws, a theory from a man who is totally depraved, spiritually discerned, and eternally cursed by God (Genesis 3:17-19). MacArthur (1995, p. 88) describes the condition of total depravity as having:

> . . . *no ability* to do spiritual good or work for their own salvation from sin. They are *so completely disinclined* to love righteousness, so *thoroughly dead* in sin, that they are *not*

able to save themselves or even to fit themselves for God's salvation. (Italics mine.)

Two, psychology teaches man is not depraved but basically good. Speaking to hundreds of Australian high school students, Weller (2002, A Road Less Walked), a former criminal, believes there is no bad student, claiming, "There is no such thing as a bad kid, only some kids who sometimes do bad things drives him in his quest to obtain successful outcomes for young people." Undoubtedly, Weller along with psychologists believed man is basically good. When a child misbehaves it does not mean he is bad. It is the lack of self-esteem that makes him bad. Building self-esteem in the child provides therapeutic cure for this mental illness (Field 1993, pp. ix, x).

However, self-esteem as an ultimate antidote to problems of living is a myth and a deception. It never cures the wickedness of the heart (Jeremiah 17: 9). Man may try to cover his wickedness with self-esteem, just like what the first man Adam did (Genesis 2: 7-10), but the sting of wickedness is still there residing in his heart. To completely remove such wickedness of the heart requires a divine operation according to the **instruction** recorded in the Bible (John 3: 3). Men's prescriptions do not work. King David said, "Wherewithal shall a young man cleanse his way? by taking heed thereto according to thy word" (Psalm 199: 9).

The *second* instruction to man is regeneration and not just change of behavior according to psychology. Since man became a sinner, he needs regeneration. In regeneration man undergoes a second birth – spiritual birth. Christ said to Nicodemus, "Jesus answered and said unto him, Verily, verily, I say unto thee, except a man be born again, he cannot see the kingdom of God" (John 3:3). To be born again is to repent from sin. It is turning away from sin and appropriate faith in the Lord Jesus Christ. Without repentance from sin (Luke 13:3) and faith in Christ (Ephesians 2:8, 9) regeneration is impossible. Repentance is an action to put an end to sinning against God permanently. Faith in Christ is a total and absolute trust that Christ alone can save him from his sin (John 3:16; Ephesians 2:8, 9).

The *third* instruction to man is the command for sanctification. Sanctification is the practice of holy living. It is the working out of believers' salvation. Sanctification is production of good works from the time of conversion until glorification (MacArthur Jr 1995, p. 130). The verses in Romans 12:1-2 touch on a life that is a **living sacrifice** and a **transformed mind**. A **transformed mind** has no business with sin. A sanctified life has put an end all activities of the flesh.

Problems of living disappear from a sanctified life. A life that is a *living sacrifice* has a heart that is settled right with God. It is not a change of behavior as what psychologists do always prescribe to their patients (Field 1993, p. 124). Psychological change involves only short-live, external change. But, sanctification involves both internal and external permanent transformation (2 Corinthians 5:17). Incidentally, sanctification is not but a product of salvation. Psychology does not change the heart. Sanctification demonstrates a transformed heart. Once a patient is in psychotherapy it would be an on-going treatment (Bulkley 1993, p. 117). However, once a sinner turns to Christ, his sin is settled before God once and for all, and now he lives a sanctified life. Once he practices holy living, problems of living or "mental illness" start to pull off until nothing is left. Result, he will experience a holy and joyful life. A sanctified life always listens to the superior instruction of the Scripture. Psalm 1: 1-2 is very clear on this matter. It says:

> Blessed is the man that walketh not in the counsel of the ungodly, nor standeth in the way of sinners, nor sitteth in the seat of the scornful. But his delight is in the law of the LORD; and in his law doth he meditate day and night.

8

Superior Expertise on Human Behavior

Secondly, that, biblical counseling has superior expertise on matters of human behavior. Psychology boasts that it has all the solutions for "mental diseases" or problems of living (Cava 1990, p. iv). Worst, psychological counseling is believed to be better than biblical counseling when the latter is integrated with the Bible (Bobgan 1987, p. 52). Psychologists contend that the Bible is not enough in dealing with mental illness (MacArthur Jr 1991, p. 108). However, all of these psychological claims are entirely baseless for the simple reason that mental illness is nonexistent, the Scriptures is incompatible with psychology, and the Bible is sufficient for all the needs of problems of living. There is no doubt the Bible has the superior expertise in dealing with problems of living. The Bible, in 2 Peter 1: 3, declares, thus:

> According as his divine power hath given unto us all things that pertain unto life and godliness, through the knowledge of him that hath called us to glory and virtue.

The above Scripture speaks of the comprehensive and sufficient expertise of the Bible on matters of problems of living. God has not left knowledge that would only keep any problems of life unsolved or provides short-term relief. He gives believers the best and the most accurate knowledge of the human heart, which produces problems of living. Bobgan (1987, p. 109) argues, "There is no book that surpasses the Bible in giving an accurate understanding of the human heart." The Bible has all the answers for problems of worry, anxiety, depression, be it mental, emotional, behavioral diseases. God's Word has all the wisdom even for the hardest human problems. In his book, "Our Sufficiency in Christ," MacArthur (1991, p. 111), strongly asserts:

> Where can we get reliable answers for life's hardest questions? Our all-sufficient Savior has not left us without ample spiritual resources. His perfect wisdom is available through His Word. Comfort, assurance, understanding, and power are ours through the ministry of His indwelling Spirit.

That, *mental illness* advocated by psychologists is nonexistent. There is no such disease known as *mental illness, disorder,* or *dysfunction.* These are coined words by psychologists. What the health professionals refer to when they mention mental illness is problems of living. Bobgan bluntly denies the existence of mental illness, (1987, p. 133), contending,

> The terms *mental disease, mental illness*, and *mental disorder* are popular catch-alls for all kinds of problems of living, most of which have little or nothing to do with disease. As soon as a person's behavior is labeled 'illness', treatment and therapy become the solutions.

If psychologists do not even know how to label exactly a real disease, how can they claim expertise in treating human behavior problems? The inevitable conclusion is, that *psychologists are no experts at all in dealing with problems of living*. They are ineffective counselors and even pose danger to the patients. Bulkley (1993, p. 73) reveals,

> The unpleasant truth is that psychology is not only relatively ineffective in changing thought and behavior patterns, but in many cases is also harmful to its clients.

Brushing aside the existence of mental illness, Bobgan (1987, pp. 133-134) distinguishes between the terms "mental" and "brain". He argues mental means "mind", and *mind* is different from *brain*. The mind is not the same as brain. Mind is the function or activity of the brain. To equate mind as equivalent to brain defies scientific facts. Mind is not a physical organ. Only physical organs can have diseases. Since mind is not a physical organ, therefore, mind cannot have *mental illness*.

There are three major reasons why psychologists do persist to use the label of *mental illness* in the course of their functions. *One*, economic security or financial enrichment. If a patient suffers no disease, there is nothing to be treated, no need of psychotherapists, and therefore, no huge payout (Bulkley 1993, pp.90-92, 112). *Two*, avoidance of responsibility before man and God. A person suffering a disease cannot be held responsible for his misbehavior (MacArthur Jr 1995, p. 21). A typical example is a person who kills another on the grounds of psychotic illness cannot be held criminally liable. Reason, such attacker is rather a casualty than a criminal. People do not like responsibility. Unbelievers cannot accept they are sinners before God. So, psychologists change the word "sin" into "mental illness, mental disease, mental disorder, or dysfunction," to avoid responsibility before God. *Three*, disobedience to God's command. Despite the clear command of the Scriptures for repentance, obedience, and sanctification, sinners rebel against God; they just want to do whatever their desires and not what God wants them to be (Romans 1:18-32).

Superior Authority Embedded in the Scriptures

Thirdly, that, biblical counseling has a superior authority embedded in the Scriptures over psychological counseling. The authority of biblical counseling is the Bible itself. Of all the books in the secular world it is the Bible that is the most practical, relevant, and life changing guide for living (Bobgan 1987, p.120). Since God cannot lie, the Bible is absolutely authoritative for all problems of living. It does not require additives from men's opinions. The Bible is absolutely authoritative and adequate for every problem of human behavior. One of the greatest preachers to Gentile nations, Apostle Paul (2 Tim 3:16-17) asserts,

> All scripture is given by inspiration of God, and is profitable for doctrine, for reproof, for correction, for *instruction* in righteousness. That the man of God may be perfect, thoroughly furnished unto all good works. (Italics mine.)

A car inventor knows the intricacies of the car, and its minutest parts, its strength and weakness. He knows better than its mechanic, driver, or passenger. When the car gets wrong the *most authoritative* person to fix it is the inventor. In the same manner, God is the Creator of man (Genesis 2:7). He knows the anatomy of man, his intricacies and his deepest secrets his strength and weakness. He knows better (John 2:24-25) the anatomy and behavior of man than any human being on the face of the earth. It appears therefore, God is the ***most authoritative*** in dealing with the problems of living. These facts can only be found in His Word – the Bible. There is no human wisdom, even that of the best of psychologists, on earth is recognized by the Scriptures as **authority** for human behavior. As a matter of fact man's best wisdom is reckoned as "foolishness" or rubbish before the eyes of God.

Apostle Paul (1 Cor. 1:19-21) lambasts human wisdom as foolish, arguing, amongst others:

> For it is written, I will destroy the wisdom of the wise, and will bring to nothing the understanding of the prudent. Where is the wise? Where is the scribe? Where is the disputer of this world? Hath not God made foolish the wisdom of this world? For after that in the wisdom of God the world by wisdom knew not God, it pleased God by the foolishness of preaching to save them that believe.

The theories and techniques of psychology are *incredulous, unscientific,* and *fictitious.* According to Bobgan these psychological theories and techniques are **psychoheresy** (Bobgan 1987, pp 7-8), claiming:

> We have chosen the term *psychoheresy* because what we describe is a psychological heresy. It is heresy because it is a departure from the fundamental truth of the Gospel. The departure is of the unproven and unscientific psychological opinions of men instead of absolute confidence in the biblical truth of God.

Hence, psychological counseling is based on human opinions and man-made philosophies. It cannot treat therapy for mental disorders without compromising the patient's life since it is no authority at all for problems of living. Furthermore, these psychological theories and techniques are often conflicting and even defy common sense understanding. They are so unreliable that one's life is at stake when psychologists deal with problems of living. Bobgan (1987, p. 206) states:

> The psychological ways of counseling are based upon man-made philosophies which teach that man is intrinsically good, that there is no personal God, that the man can rise above his circumstances and become his own standard of right and wrong. Most Christians who practice psychology would not agree with one of the most basic premises of psychological theories: that man can become a better human being without God.

That is exactly the case when man's assorted wisdom becomes the basic criterion for human behavior for it is no standard at all. It cannot be taken as standard of authority. It is not like biblical counseling that there is a clear-cut standard of authority – the Scripture itself for every aspect of human behavior.

Superior Cure for Problems of Living

Fourthly, that, biblical counseling has a superior cure for problems of living. While the Bible does not mention the words "mental illness," it is the only book that has more something to say about *problems* and *cure* of human behavior than any other book on earth. The Scripture records the perfect and purest human behavior that ever existed on this planet until the time it was ruined by sin. Problems of living, evils in society, any environmental and human problems are due to one direct cause – the sin that entered into this world through the first man Adam (Genesis 3:9-19). Before Adam's disobedience, everything was perfect, beautiful, and "very good." After his disobedience, everything was cursed and ruined. Inorganic or genetic problems, human and environmental catastrophic consequences started to occur (Rom. 8:22). Had the first man not disobeyed God, there is no such thing as **problems of living**. Adams (Institute for Nouthetic Studies) writes,

> All problems stem from Adam's sin. Had there been no fall, there would be no remedial counseling. But Adam *did* sin, and if you were to trace genetic problems, environmental factors, and poor training back far enough, you would discover that it is because of the fall that these problems exist. Sin, then, rather than being a limiting concept, is the broadest of all. It covers the waterfront!

To completely provide lasting cure for problems of living once and for all is to basically deal with the cause of the problems, that is, sin. Man needs to know that ignoring sin in his life cannot solve all his problems of living. Sin of the heart should be settled first before problems of living can be treated. Every sinner has to admit he is a sinner and needs to be saved through faith in Christ (John 3:3). Living a sinful life causes mental-emotional-behavioral problems (Bobgan 1987). The only solution for this is restoring the patient's life to God through repentance of sin and faith in the Lord Jesus Christ. Bobgan (1987, p. 219) points out,

> A Christian who counsels biblically knows that sin must be dealt with, just a doctor knows that cancer should not be simply redefined or ignored. Confession and repentance bring about restoration and that is what is Christian counseling is all about.

God's Word provides a long lasting effect of cure from problems of living such as alcoholism. It is only the Lord Jesus Christ who can transform the life of a drug addict, an alcoholic, a prostitute and others from the mire of sin. Bobgan (1987, p. 109) assures, "There is no one else who can transform a life like Jesus can." While in therapies, he spent years, yet they only provide short-term relief. God's Word is powerful, it transforms a useless, cast-out alcoholic into a useful, humble member of God's kingdom, with a completely cured life from problems of living from the moment of faith in Christ (2 Corinthians 5:17). The Bible says, "For the Word of God is quick, and powerful, and sharper than any two edged sword, piercing even to the dividing asunder of soul and spirit, and of the joints and marrow, and is a discerner of the thoughts and intents of the heart" (Hebrews 4:12). There is no doubt God has provided a long lasting cure for every problem of human behaviour through repentance, confession, forgiveness of sin, sanctification, and faith in Christ.

Superior Evidence of Transformed and Cured Lives

Fifthly, that, biblical counseling has a superior evidence of transformed and cured lives from problems of living. Psychology boasts of its evidence of cured patients based on fictitious statistics of psychologists. The claim of successes have been well publicized in books or newspapers that ordinary people do not notice the overwhelming evidence of therapeutic failures that are buried undocumented. In the introduction of her book on self-esteem, Field (1993, p. xi) promotes self-esteem to be the key factor in solving mental illness, claiming, amongst others:

> In nearly all fields of counseling, the development of self-esteem is now recognized as the key factor in positive self development. With the help of my clients I have developed many methods to increase self-esteem and eventually I brought all the techniques together to make this book. Because we are all different, with a unique set of strengths and weaknesses, there are techniques to suit each one of us, whatever the occasion and whatever 'types' of person we are. In whichever area of your life you feel you need support, you will find the necessary tools to help you in this book.

18

She believes all evidence of success in developing self-esteem is provided in her book for any type of people. Any innocent person would be led to believe by mere reading of this book that creating self-esteem is 100% panacea against *mental illness*.

In another instance, LaHaye (1984, p. 9-10) boasts that knowing one's temperaments and analyzing that of others serve as the key to maximize one's potential. He advanced the *four-temperament theory*, contending,

> Temperament influences everything you do – from sleep habits to study habits to eating style to the way you get with other people. Humanly speaking, there is no other influence in your life more powerful than your temperament or combination of temperaments. That is why it is so essential to know your temperament and to be able to analyze other people's temperaments, not to condemn them, but so you can maximize your potential and enable them to maximize theirs.

Definitely LaHaye is saying, one should not worry about his suffering from drug addiction since by knowing his temperament, everything will be gone. But these claims of psychological successes do suffer consternation for they are more speculations than real. Scientific evidence shows that psychology brings therapeutic effect no better than no therapy at all. In his criticism of psychological therapeutic effect Zimbardo (1988, p. 591) admits:

> For unknown reasons, some percentage of mental patients improve without any professional intervention. This spontaneous recovery effect is the baseline against which the 'cure rate' of therapies must be assessed. Simply put, doing something must be shown to lead to significantly greater percentage of improved cases than doing nothing, or just letting time pass. As is often the case with physical ailments, many psychological problems improve because time heals all (or a reasonable proportion of) wounds.

Thus, psychological counseling cannot be trusted in dealing with problems of living for it is no better than without therapy at all.

However, counseling from the Bible demonstrates superior evidence over psychotherapy. The reason for this is obvious. God is all powerful (Matthew 28:18) there is no disease that is not curable in Him. With God there is no problem of living that is impossible to cure (Luke 1:37). A remarkable evidence of absolute cure is the demonic insane man recorded in Mark 5:1-19 healed by Christ. Mark records this incident and other people including his parents noticed the healing of former insane man to be now indisputably permanent, normal and in *his right mind*. Another instance is a Samaritan woman (John 4:4-30) who suffers from sexual disease saw Jesus, believed on

Him, she was transformed and later became a faithful witness for Christ. Apostle Paul before his conversion suffered from certain psychotic disease, which enabled him to nab and murder Christians (Acts 7:58 - 8:1-3; 9:1-2). But God saved Paul from sin and completely cured his problems of living, he later became one of the staunch and greatest preachers to the Gentiles (Acts 9:3-15). And, throughout the centuries tens of thousands and multitude of people suffering all kinds of problems of living have been cured and transformed into the image of Christ. Thus, there is no doubt biblical counseling provides healing better than psychology.

Superior Product of Transformed Lives

Finally, that, biblical counseling produces a superior product of transformed lives. Down through the ages, Christians, those who were healed by Christ have been the most hated people (John 17:14; 15:17-19) on earth and yet, the most respectful people to authorities and fellowmen, and have been noble citizens (Romans 13:1-7). To illustrate this point, Paul and Silas (Acts 16:16-40) were arrested and jailed for preaching the gospel at Philippi. At midnight while they were praying and singing gospel songs, and at the time the jailor was asleep, an earthquake occurred, the jail was broken, a chance for any prisoners to escape. But the prisoners Paul and Silas remained inside the jail. The Philippian jailor was awakened with the jail broken, unsheathed his sword ready to commit suicide for fearing his prisoners Paul and Silas had already escaped and to avoid criminal responsibility. Noticing the death intent of the jail guard, Paul yelled, "Do thyself no harm: for we are all here," to stop him from killing himself. The jail guard kneeled down before Paul and Silas and said "Sirs, what must I do to be saved?" Paul led him to believe on Christ. As a result, the Philippian jail guard got saved and has been transformed and cured permanently from *homicidal illness*. This incident led to the salvation of jailor's family.

However, results from psychological counseling are of poor quality, most of them get worse, disrespectful to authorities, fake, fraud, and criminals. The following report is quite alarming. Psychologists Simon, Irvin, and Drinnin (1987, p. 565) unanimously concur that patients under therapy get worse, admitting:

> Many studies support the idea that therapy is quite capable of producing harm. Studies of group therapy clients indicate that a small percentage of the group members are worse off after treatment than before treatment and that *the results can be traced to therapy*. Even during therapy, some clients become psychotic, commit suicide, or become so mentally ill they need hospitalization . . . (Italics mine.)

Conclusion

In view of the foregoing circumstances ***there is no reason to believe*** that biblical counseling is not superior over psychological counseling. *One*, that, biblical counseling has a superior Bible-based instruction. God's Word never fabricates theories and lies. Psychology is full of conflicting opinions with contradicting theories and techniques. God initially prescribes one instruction to guarantee freedom from all sorts of problems of living. But man decided to disobey God. Hence, all sorts of problems of living started to crop up.

Two, that, biblical counseling has a superior expertise of the problems of living. Since God created man, He knows exactly the right solution for every problem of human behavior. No therapist or psychologist has that equal caliber to know the intricacies of the science of the mind. Problems of living fall within the province of spiritual wisdom and are beyond the reach of psychologists. The science of the mind is the proper jurisdiction of God.

Three, that, biblical counseling has a superior authority in matters of problems of living. Since human behavior touches the spiritual side of man, no one except God has the authority to deal with his problems.

Psychologists may try but it is an exercise in futility since they have no power and authority to do the job.

Four, that, biblical counseling has a superior cure of the problems of living. God's Word has demonstrated its long lasting effect in dealing with problems of human behavior. Psychology may give short-term relief but it fails to deliver its cure once and for all. The worse scenario is that it never cures at all.

Five, that biblical counseling has a superior evidence of cured and transformed lives. Thousands upon thousands of lives have been demonstrated to have been cured and delivered permanently from the clutches of sin, not to mention problems of living. Psychology presents a few relapsing evidence which is even tainted with worse results than before therapy.

Finally, that, biblical counseling has a superior product of transformed lives. It means that products from biblical counseling produce superior and quality results. While products of psychology have been characterized to be of poor quality. It fails to produce respectful and noble citizens. When therapy gets worst which is the rule rather than the exception its results are characterized with people who are fake, fraudulent, disrespectful to humanity, criminals and eventually become problems of society. Accordingly, in spite of the allegation that psychology is scientific, its dream as a panacea of mental illness or problems of living remains a fantasy.

References

__________, 2000, <u>KJV Giant Printer Center Column Reference Bible</u>, Zondervan Publishing House, Grand Rapids, Michigan.

Adams, Jay, n.d., "You Talk About Nothing Else But Sin," [Online], Available: http://www.nouthetic.org/Obj-sin.html [2002, December 24].

Bobgan, Martin and Deidre, 1987, <u>Psychoheresy: The Psychological Seduction of Christianity</u>, East Gate Publishers, Santa Barbara, California.

Bobgan, Martin and Deidre, n.d., "The Psychoanalytic Stream of Psychology Freud's Legacy to 'Christian Psychology'," [Online], Available: http://www.psychoheresy-aware.org/freudl36.html [2002, December 17].

Bulkley, Ed, 1993, <u>Why Christians Can't Trust Psychology</u>, Harvest House Publishers, Eugene, Oregon.

Cava, Roberta, 1990, <u>Dealing with Difficult People</u>, 2000, Reprint, Judy Piatkus Ltd, London.

Field, Lynda, 1993, <u>Creating Self-Esteem</u>, Element, Rockport, Massachusetts.

LaHaye, Tim, 1984, <u>Why You Act The Way You Do</u>, Living Books, Wheaton, Illinois.

MacArthur Jr, John, F., 1991, <u>Our Sufficiency In Christ</u>, Crossway Books, Wheaton, Illinois.

MacArthur Jr, John, F., 1995, The Vanishing Conscience: Drawing The Line In A No-Fault, Guilt-Free World, Word Publishing, Dallas.

Miesel, Rick, ed., 2001, "Counseling Methods Survey: Theories/Theorists & Terminology," [Online],

Available:
http://www.rapidnet.com/~jbeard/bdm/

Psychology/ [2002, December 17].

Simons, Janet A., et. Al., 1987, <u>Psychology: The Search For Understanding</u>, West Publishing Company, New York.

Weller, Dallas, 2002, "A Road Less Walked," Eastern Goldfields Senior High School, Kalgoorlie, WA, Australia.

Zimbado, Philip G., 1988, <u>Psychology and Life</u>, 12th Ed., Scott, Foresman and Company, Glenview, Illinois.

Bibliography

Andrews, Michael, 1976, <u>The Life that Lives on Man,</u> Taplinger Publishing Co., Inc., New York.

Birch, Charles, 1995, <u>Feelings,</u> University of New South Wales Press, Sydney.

Branden, Nathaniel, 1994, <u>The Six Pillars of Self-Esteem</u>, Bantam Books, New York.

Carlson, Neil R., 1988, <u>Discovering Psychology</u>, Allyn and Bacon, Inc., Boston.

Cole, Steven J., 1993, "Questions & Answers," [Online], Available: http://www.psychoheresy-aware.org/questions.html [2002, December 17].

Coleman, James C., et. al, 1987, <u>Contemporary Psychology and Effective Behavior</u>, 6th ed., Scott, Foresman and Company, Dallas, Texas.

Corsini, Raymond J., ed., 1994, <u>Encyclopedia of Psychology</u>, 2nd ed., John Wiley & Sons, New York.

Dann, Jill, 2001, <u>Understanding Emotional Intelligence</u>, Hodler & Stoughton, London.

Davies, Jean, 1997, <u>Choice in Dying</u>, Ward Lock Wellington House, London.

Faelten, Sharon, et. al, 1988, <u>Take Control of Your Life: A Complete Guide to Stress Relief</u>, Rodale Press, Inc. Emmaus, Pennsylvania.

Fennell, Melanie J.V., 1999, <u>Overcoming Low Self-Esteem: A Self-help Guide Using Behavioral Techniques</u>, Robinson Publishing Ltd, London.

Goldberg, Michael, 1997, 9 Personality Types: The Ennegram for Success at Work, Thornsons, London.

Hernacki, Mike, 1990, The Secret of Conquering Fear, Pelican Publishing Company, Gretna, Louisiana.

Hogg, Michael A., et. Al, eds., 1993, Group Motivation: Social Psychological Perspective, Harvester Wheat sheaf, New York.

Janes, William, 1952, The Principles of Psychology, 30th Printing, Encyclopaedia Britannica, Inc. Chicago.

Jeffers, Susan, 1999, I'm Okay You're A Brat, Hodder Headline Australia Pty Ltd, Sydney.

Kurtz, Paul, ed., 1985, A Skeptic's Handbook of Parapsychology, Prometheus Books, Buffalo, New York.

MacArthur Jr, John F., 1993, Ashamed of the Gospel: When The Church Becomes Like The World, Crossway Books, Wheaton, Illinois.

Makinde, Olu, 1983, Fundamentals of Guidance and Counseling, MacMillan Publishers, London.

Mandelbaum, W. Adam, 2000, The Psychic Battlefield: A History of the Military – Occult Complex, St. Martin's Press, New York.

Prager, Dennis, 1998, Happiness Is a Serious Problem: A Human Nature Repair Manual, Regan Books, New York.

Sharpe, Robert, 1984, Thrive on Stress, Souvenir Press Ltd, London.

Stevens, Laurence, "Does Mental Illness Exist?", [Online], Available:

http://www.antipsychiatry.org/exist.htm [2002, December 17].

Tieger, Paul D., et. al, 2001, <u>Do What You Are</u>, 3rd ed., Scribe Publications, Melbourne.

Turner, Jeffrey S., et. al, 1991, <u>Lifespan Development</u>, 4th ed., Holt, Rinehart Winston, Inc., Chicago.

Westcott, Patsy, 1995, <u>The Survivor Personality, Bloombury Publishing Plc, London.</u>

White, Kate, ed., 1998, <u>9 Secrets of Women Who Get Everything They Want</u>, Harmony Books, New York.

Wilson, Glenn, ed., 1989, <u>Your Personality & Potential</u>, Salem House Publishers, Topsfield, Massachusetts.

Wilson, John A.R., et. al, 1969, <u>Psychological Foundations of Learning and Teaching</u>, McGraw-Hill Book Company, New York.

Wollheinn, Richard, 1991, <u>Freud</u>, 2nd ed., Fontana Press, London.

CHAPTER 2

According to Martin and Deidre Bobgan's Book – Psychoheresy: The Psychological Seduction of Christianity

Leaven in the Loaf

Psychoheresy is a book written by Martin and Deidre Bobgan. In Chapter 1, "Leaven in the Loaf", opens the book by saying that psychology has infiltrated the pulpit and the church teaching satanic theories, unproven and unscientific techniques. Basically, the book starts by defining and explaining what leaven is, psychoheresy, Christian psychology, psychological seduction, and myths of psychology. The "leaven" which is now penetrating the church pulpit refers to psychology. Psychology is very subtle and so persuasive that even pastors and preachers do not notice they are already victims of psychology. Now, merging psychological theories and the Scriptures is a blatant slap on Biblical principles. These two are incompatible. Psychology has been authored by the Devil, and the Bible had been inspired by God.

Psychoheresy refers to psychological theories and techniques. These are known as heresy because science fails to present evidence to support it. The

Bible rejects psychological theories and techniques. Psychology can hardly be documented with scientific facts. All of its theories and techniques are mere allegations they are more fantasy than real.

Christian psychologists would prefer to see a believer who practices psychology. He believes psychological theories can be applied to Christians. This is contrary to the teaching of the Scriptures on separation. The Christian psychologist believes that he is even more qualified and better equip to practice psychology than the unredeemed psychologist for the simple reason that he is a Christian who knows both Bible principles and psychological theories. Hence, Christians are seduced believing psychology is a better cure than the Bible. As a result, many Christians would rather see a psychologist than the pastor or fellow believers. The pastor is only good in spiritual matters.

There are four major myths or theories of psychology. *Firstly*, that psychotherapy is science rather than religion. Psychotherapy refers to the theories and techniques used in psychological counseling. Since psychological counseling uses some so-called scientific methods it is assumed as science. Knowing that psychotherapy is not religion, there is no competition with the pastor. This is where the pastor is caught off-guard without knowing his members are already psychologically seduced.

Secondly, that the merging of Bible and psychology present the best kind of counseling. This is hinged on the theory that the integration of Bible and psychology would bring about a better cure. It theorizes that Christian psychologists are the best psychological counselors since they have got the Word of God who trained on biblical principles. This makes unredeemed psychologists inferior to Christian psychologists.

Thirdly, that people experiencing "mental-emotional-behavioral" disturbances are *mentally ill*. Mental illness is a psychological illness and hence, they need psychological counselors. The pastor is not qualified to deal with emotional illness in the sense that it is not a spiritual problem. The pastor can only deal with spiritual conflict.

Fourthly, that there exists a high rate of success in psychotherapy. Dealing with emotional problems can have a high chance to be solved by professional psychological counselors than by biblical counselors. This is for the simple reason that psychologists or psychotherapists have been properly and professionally trained in psychology. Biblical counselors are not trained for the job.

In spite of these psychological theories, the Bible rejects them absolutely. The only source of genuine, scientific, and professional counseling is God and His Word.

Psychology as Religion

Psychology is not science. It is a religion. Science is just used to disguise its procedures and theories to attract people and its customers. Psychology is rather a religion in the sense that it uses its methods and tactics to deceive the innocent ones. It is using methods and techniques that are beyond the bounds of scientific test. Examples of these are: hypnosis, psychoanalysis, familiar spirits or archetypes, mind control, mind over matter, mesmerisms, faith healing, and many others.

Human behavior is deeply embedded in the Scriptures from Genesis to Revelation. The Bible records why and how man behaves that way. It lists problems, conflicts, and solutions for human behavior. Since the Bible deals with lots of behavior problems with appropriate solutions, it is rather a better authority in behavior counseling than psychology or psychotherapy.

Strictly speaking, any fields that deals with the "why's" and "how's" of human behavior – attitudes, morals, and values, is a mantle of religion. Religion seeks to heal psychic illness, wrong behavior, low morality, deteriorating values, emotional disturbance or stress, and other individual dysfunctions.

Psychology is a product of rejecting the Creator and disobeying Scriptural principles or commands. This is very clear from the lives of those recognized as authorities in psychology, particularly, Segmund Freud and Carl Jung. Freud developed utter disregard of God and hatred to Christians. He believes God and His people cause all problems of humanity. Jung rejected the religion of his parents but admitted the theory that religion is the solution to life's problems. Hence, psychology becomes the root of alternatives of religion. Therefore, psychology is an act of defiance against God's authority to heal.

Another individual who is very popular in psychology is Franz Anton Mesmer who developed psychological theories and techniques ahead of Freud and Jung. Mesmer's theories are known as Mesmerism, which is based on the theory that the human body contains an "invisible fluid". He renamed this fluid as "animal magnetism." Animal magnetism is simply the belief that a human body has an invisible fluid in that when it is properly distributed, it solves behavior problems or psychotic illnesses. Mesmerism has been adopted in psychology as an effective tool against psychological dysfunctions. One of its known techniques utilized by psychological counselors is hypnosis. Along with hypnosis, the techniques – telepathy, precognition, clairvoyance, psychotherapy, and positive thinking were developed. These techniques are part and parcel of occult activities.

Psychology deals with "cure of minds" rather than "cure of souls." To a psychotherapist, sin is considered psychological or mind illness. This is contrary to the facts revealed in Scriptures. Sin is a problem of the heart as a result of man's wrong act committed against God. There is no possible cure for sin except repentance from sin and turning towards God.

Transpersonal is a form of psychotherapy that is the most religious amongst the techniques reported to by psychotherapists. It believes in a "supernatural" demonic spirits. This is one of the techniques that has close references to occult activities. Healing cannot be done without the "suggestions" of demonic spirits.

Christianity is more than psychology or religion. It is a relationship to God through faith in Christ. Once a sinner turns to Christ, his so-called "psychological dysfunction" is cured once and for all. He does not need psychotherapists to cure his sin. He needs no other but Christ for He is the great Healer of all diseases – organic or spiritual.

Science of Pseudoscience

Psychology has a remote possibility that it can be classified as science. The reason is that psychology is based primarily on unscientific views, opinions, false theories of unregenerate men and women. Psychology rather presents confusion, contradictions, scientific facade, and psychological entrenchment to its victims. Psychotherapy tries to explain of unacceptable behavior by adopting methods of scientific enquiry. It theorizes that human problems can be explained scientifically. However, the result of studies defies the wishes of psychology. Its ambition to be classified science is very far. Psychological history persists a "ritualistic endeavor to emulate the forms of science," one that is outside the reign of scientific laws. All of its so-called "psychological facts" have been rendered negative against the test of scientific investigation.

Statements of psychologists are mere opinions and not facts. When psychologists or psychotherapists move from describing the event to explaining or changing it, they are moving from fact to fiction. A classic example of this is the Stockholm Syndrome. Observers describe that in hostage robberies, the victims are more protective of their captors rather than cooperate with the police officers. Expert psychologists or psychotherapists try to explain this phenomenon as influenced by the behavior of the victims when they were infants. The mother supports her infant of its needs. She protects her infant from the outside world. This explanation cannot stand against scientific investigation. Psychologists may have explanations why the Stockholm Syndrome behaves that way. Hence, a solid evidence to raise psychology within the realm of science remains in doubt.

Rather, psychology or psychotherapy can be classified as pseudoscience. Anything that is held to be true, but cannot pass through scientific tests is false theory, and hence, a pseudoscience. Psychology uses all available tools in scientific investigation in order to call it science. Since it cannot pass scientific tests it is pregnant with contradictory theories and techniques, and false assumptions. Genuine science has a uniform conclusion and can be tested scientifically at any time. Had psychology been scientifically proved, there is only one uniform result for human behavior or problems of living.

Instead of delivering the right cure of behavior problems psychology confuses it. Psychotherapists present many theories, techniques, and explanations of life's problems. They even indicate that parents, stars, bio-chemical make-up, diet, life-style, and "kharma" of the past cause children's problems. Rather than describing problems of living in one uniform cause scientifically, psychologists side tract the sufferers to other unscientific explanations.

Another group of people who seem to be convincing is the Christian psychologists. This group believes that "all truth is God's truth". To them the truth of the Bible and the truth of psychology are similar. These truths can be mixed or amalgamated into one since they are the same. So, whatever is true to psychotherapy is also true in the Bible. Hence, there is integration of theology and psychology. This means that God and psychologists such as Freud, Jung, Roger, or B.F. Skinner are compatible. This is a false theory. God and Satan are incompatible from the beginning. Thus, psychological theories and techniques do not work with God.

The pseudo-scientific nature of psychology or psychotherapy is a scientific façade. It is not real science. It has its origins in myths or astrology. Psychology presents myths or astrology as facts that are beyond the bounds of as science. They are beyond scientific research. Its tenets defy the nature of science, which is reputable, predictable, reproducible, and contradictable.

Promises, Promises, Promises

There are lots of promises and advertisements in psychotherapy. This is naturally expected if one has to attract customers. Quick fix and complete healing are the usual approaches utilized by psychotherapists to their clients. Below are some examples of these promises.

In the secular world, the Cambridge – Somerville Youth Study is a classic example of promises to get cured from problems of living that provides no cure at all. A group of 650 boys between the ages of six and ten were chosen for study who had high risk of becoming delinquents. These boys were divided into two groups – the treated group, and the control group. The treated group was subjected to psychotherapy for at least an average of five years. The control group was left untreated – no psychotherapy was administered. At the conclusion of the study the psychotherapists claimed great success. This indicates that the treated group was cured from becoming delinquents or criminals.

However, a follow-up study was conducted to verify the claim of the psychotherapists. The result of this follow-up was disturbing. The treated group, the ones that received psychotherapy for five years, was worse than the control group, one who did not receive any treatment. It indicates that the treated group were more delinquent, and potential criminals. Without verification through scientific investigation the psychotherapist's claim of great success for complete cure from problems of living is quite staggering.

Promises of psychotherapy cure do not only abound in secular world but it also is prevalent in the Christian community. A book by William Bakers (Clinical psychologist) and Marie Chapian (Psychotherapist) promotes promises by Misbelief Therapy. Misbelief Therapy offers universal cure for problems of living. It uses cognitive therapy and biblical ideas. It guarantees healing of life's problems regardless of circumstances. This psychotherapy technique is based on Proverbs 23:7. Bakers and Chapian do interpret this verse that as long as the sufferer changes his thoughts, he can attain whatever he desires. But, this interpretation of Proverbs 23:7 violates the significant hermeneutic principle of contextual construction. This verse should not be left isolated when trying to interpret its meaning. Its context includes verses 6 and 8. Verses 6, 7, and 8 of Proverbs 23 teach warning about trusting someone based on outward appearance. Proverbs 23:7 cannot be used to support one's change of behavior and desires. Otherwise, it is misapplying Scriptures.

The next example appeared in Christian magazines. Christian clinical psychologist Martha

Rogers, in her article "A Family in Crisis," describes psychotherapists can have four approaches to problems of living. These are: biblical approach (Nouthetic Counseling) and the three psychological approaches which are behavioral, psychoanalytic, and systems therapies. She favors the systems therapy approach to be beneficial for family problems. The husband's depression according to Rogers was cured. His problem of drinking alcohol was solved. The couples enjoy each other more than before. In the absence of scientific investigation systems therapy appears to be a real help to family problems.

Let the sufferers or people having problems of living be warned. The investigation on therapy improvement does not warrant the promises made in books, magazines, workshops, talks, tapes and ads advocated by therapists and practitioners, Christians or unbelievers. The claim that therapy plus the Bible presents better cure rather than the Bible alone falls short of facts. The Bible alone, the sole basis of biblical counseling, without adulteration is a simple cure of souls.

Amalgamania

Amalgamation is integration of the Bible and psychology or psychotherapy and is described in Chapter 5. Psychological influences do not only exist in secular world but have already traversed the portals of Christian Churches. These influences are apparent in at least nine different cases. *One*, there exists psychologized preaching. The constant reference to psychologists or psychotherapists as authorities for problems of living in the pulpit by pastors and preachers is indicative of this phenomenon. *Two*, psychologized church counseling. The church counselors argue the Bible is not enough to meet the needs of Christians dealing with problems of living. *Three*, church assistants are psychologically trained rather than trained from the principles of Scriptures. *Four*, when church members ask the pastor for counseling they are referred to professional psychological counselors. *Five*, there exists rising numbers of churches providing licensed psychological counselors. *Six*, Christian institutions rely on psychological techniques instead of biblical principles. *Seven*, at conferences it is required the presence of psychological counselors. *Eight*, an increasing number of selected individuals to review books about helping life's problem tend to be psychological rather than biblical. *Finally*, the growing number of books, tapes, workshops, talks, and seminars tend to be psychological.

Many pastors advocate the amalgamation of psychology and the Bible. Richard Dobbins, a minister, envisioned to Christianize psychology by welding together psychology and theology. But, he ended up psychologizing the church by adapting the tenets of humanistic psychology. He advocated a psychotherapy theory, the hydraulic model. This model states if anger is held, it hurts; if released, it helps. Hydraulic model is contrary to science and the Scriptures.

Other advocates of amalgamation of theology and psychology are Norman Wright, Laurence Crabb, Jr., Paul Tournier, M. Scott Peck, H. Newton Malony, Joseph Palotta, Cecil Osborne, Charles Solomon, and many others. These psychologists contend that both psychology and the Bible can solve problems of living. Normal Wright, a pastor promotes psychological opinions rather than God. Laurence Crabb, Jr. criticizes those who use the Scriptures solely for counseling mental-emotional-behavioral problems of living as "nothing buttery." Paul Tournier admits psychotherapy is not science; hence, one can resort to any techniques, intuition, theories of others, a bit of the Bible. M. Scott Pack defines original sin as human laziness. He believes the unconscious part of every person is God. H. Newton Malony uses Transactional Analysis developed by Thomas Harris who advocated that if one decides to be OK, then he is OK. Thomas Harris along with others has distorted biblical principles. Spiritual problems such as problems of living can never be solved at the guise of one's caprices and will. Man has no power to be OK outside of Christ. Joseph Palotta, a Christian, mixes hypnosis and psychological stages of development taught by Freud. He believes Freud's unscientific theory of Oedipus Complex model. Cecil Osborne adopts Arthur Janov's theory of Primal Therapy. The theory states that individual's problems are caused in childhood, which results to neurosis. Primal Therapy requires a return to the early years of life. Charles Solomon theorized Rejection Syndrome, a similar theory to that of Joseph Palotta. He claims that majority of mental and emotional problems can be traced to childhood rejection.

Amidst, these psychological theories and techniques, solution to problems of living remains unsolved and tends to grow worse. Until and unless psychologists and psychotherapists humble and return to the cure of souls – God's pure Word, there is no apparent solution to the problems of living.

A Way that Seemeth Right

This chapter describes psychology or psychotherapy seemingly right since it mixes or integrates with the Bible. Reading the Bible through psychological lens leads biblical principles to compromise with psychology. The amalgamation of two opposite forces – the Bible and psychology paves the way for the best cure. Each psychological counselor is free to pick and choose from over often-contradicting 250 psychological approaches, and over incompatible 10,000 psychological techniques to integrate with the Scriptures. So the church espouses these approaches and techniques in the belief that the Bible is not enough to meet the needs of Christians.

Professionalism in counseling has been the trend of today's world. The professionals have been invading the family to do the responsibilities of parents from time immemorial. Result, the sufferers have less trust if not nothing at all on persons who are not professionals such as pastors to deal with behavior problems. The psychologist has robbed the Christian's faith and God's Word for comfort in that even a simple problem he needs a professional psychologist instead of solving it by himself. Psychological therapy motivates one to depend on it, at worst it adds more problems of living than eliminating them. Thus, psychology or psychotherapy becomes the disease itself instead of cure.

The effect of psychotherapy has not only hit the church but also spread its tentacles to the members of the church. Whenever a member has a problem he tends to call the professional psychologist rather than his pastor. Psychologists replace the long time role of pastors in the area of counseling of problems of living. This is because, as Loriene Chase puts it, pastors can only deal with ecclesiastical and spiritual matters but unfit to counsel with problems of living if not psychologically trained. Chase does not recognize biblical authority on problems of the human heart, soul, mind, and behavior. To counsel problems of living the pastor should be trained and qualified to deal with "deeply rooted, life-crippling psychological problems." Mary Vander Goot, psychology professor at a Christian College said that the minister of the gospel is not qualified to counsel his members because pastor and therapist are incompatible roles. This is a difficult statement to hold since the church has survived throughout the ages before the rise of psychologists and psychotherapists.

The psychologists spread rumors that people get more harmed by pastoral or biblical counseling. This report is undocumented and scientifically verifiable. It will cause church members and others to have no trust of pastors to deal with behavior dysfunctions. Psychotherapists or psychologists do blind the eye of the public by displaying their psychological qualifications, academic titles, and their gullible promises of quick fix or complete cure. However, God's Word has not diminished its power against the problems of living. The Bible, if studied prayerfully and faithfully, has the power to deal with all problems of living.

Psychological antagonism to Christian faith is very subtle. Instead of directly and openly opposing biblical principles, psychologists put them alongside with their unscientific, self-serving opinions. They do not deny outright the validity of God's Word but simply disqualify ministers of the gospel to deal with deep, crippling mental-emotional-behavioral problems.

Evangelicalism observes there is a dramatic shift from a conservative to a liberal view of the Scriptures in the last 50 years. This is a change from theology of life to a psychology of life. Ideal of psychology creeps into theology, to the pulpit preaching positive thinking and success gospels only, thereby avoiding negative preaching such as sin, guilt, damnation in hell, and others. The message at modern times is, "fulfill yourself, do it all, have it all, in a Christian way."

48

Broken Cisterns or Living Waters

In psychology man is elevated to the position of God and man becomes god himself. This is idolatry in the form of psychotherapy. Psychology tries to invent a psychological model of God rather than a biblical model of God. Self is enthroned and God is dethroned. Psychology tries to explain the cause of man's problems in various ways other than the fall of man to sin. Bible words such as sin is replaced with less convicting and more comforting of "short-coming, mistake, relapse, or reaction to past hurt". The words "sanctified" and "holy" are substituted with "healed" and "whole", and other words of similar import. Since psychology indoctrinates self, man is highly honored. When one does not regard himself highly he is said to be suffering from mental problems. This is in direct contrast with Biblical teaching that when self is elevated to the position where God is, it is pride. To regard the self highly is pride and it is sin. One needs to humble and repent of his sin first before God can effect healing from problems of living.

Psychological idolatry has penetrated the church in the form of psychological theories and therapies. It has destroyed men's faith in God in a subtle way. Psychological idolatry is not easy to identify. In biblical times Israel's idolatry is easy to see. But psychological idolatry is so subtle in such a way that Christians who are not rooted in the Word of God can hardly realize they are already doing it. Psychological idolatry is hard to distinguish when it wears the garb of science. People know that genuine science is truth. Genuine science does not contradict the Bible. Biblical lenses fail miserable when the so-called "Christian psychologists" practice psychological idolatry.

The Scripture is the sole authority in all matters of faith and practice. It is the fountain of life, life-refreshing, and life-changing source. The Bible is embedded with tested principles, variety of human experiences, and problems applied and practiced at any stages of human life. By this there is no question the Bible is the most relevant, practical book of life. It is a textbook for physical and spiritual needs. Psychologists are wrong when they claim the Scripture only applies to spiritual matters. In fact, psychology is concerned with the "mind or psyche" of man. The "psyche" of soul and all its concerns are spiritual matters. As a matter of fact any concerns for understanding the human personality is a study of the spiritual aspect of man. To understand human personality is God's sole and exclusive jurisdiction. He does not share it to anyone or to any thing. Any attempt or intrusion to this role is but an exercise in futility. Psychology has invaded this spiritual boundary in the attempt to solve human misery. Psychologists and therapies are no solutions to problems of livimg. It is turning from sin and faith towards God that brings solution to problems of living. This fact has been demonstrated by Christians throughout the centuries ahead the rise of psychotherapists or psychologists. Every time the Christians of old experienced any human sufferings they turned to God. As a result they were healed, comforted and experienced lasting joy.

The Bible has constantly warned of consequences when God's Word is not followed. Throughout history Israel has been always warned to turn away from sin and from following the customs and gods of the nations around them. They failed many times to heed this call and they experienced consequences of their actions resulting in human problems and misery. But when they turned to God from sin, they were healed and refreshed completely.

The Misnomer of Mental Illness

In Chapter 1 the psychologists or psychotherapists misuse some medical terms or have misunderstood some medical words. A classic example is the words "mental illness". To psychologists any diseases that fall within the magic words ***mental illness*** they are quick to remark, treatment and therapy is the solution for the disease. They do not know the meaning of the incompatible words "mental illness".

The word "mental" means "mind". Mind is not the same as the brain although the former speaks of something that occurs in the brain. The mind is more than matter and more than a by-product of the brain. Mind is not a physical organ and it cannot have disease. It is wrong to say "mental illness" to someone who suffers brain disease or bad behavior. So one who suffers mental-emotional-behavioral symptoms is not "mentally ill." He is rather "medically ill."

The Bible describes man to be created with human dignity high above the level of physical organism. God created man capable of thinking, knowing, judging, and directing completely different from animals. Man is created in God's image with a human mind to know, love, trust and obey his Creator. Since God created the human mind beyond the bounds of physical realm, it goes beyond the jurisdiction of science, not to mention psychology, which is not science. Therefore, the human mind cannot be medically ill.

No psychologist, psychotherapist or even a medical practitioner is needed for the human mind. While it is true the human mind may either be redeemed or unredeemed, it gets ill. When this occurs no one is qualified to treat the disease except God. Since God created man He is the only One who knows the correct cure for whatever sorts of problems of living a man has. Though allegedly psychologists deal with "psyche" or "mind" of man, they do not operate with "brain" illnesses. They are not per se psychotherapists or medical practitioners that deal with human diseases but are teachers who teach new ways of *thinking, feeling,* and *behaving* to effect change of human behavior.

The psychologists's constant use of the words **mental disease, mental illness, mental disorder,** and **dysfunction** to refer to behavioral diseases is a misnomer. They just insist in using these terms to advance their cause and to confuse the public. Using of these terms is very clear from the following illustrations.

Ann Landers received a letter from a man who is a pedophilia complaining that homosexuals can find outlets to satisfy their desires but nothing from pedophilia people. The man is 40 years old, has four boys, and a professional accountant. He confessed he is attracted badly to little girls. Here, Landers correctly diagnosed him to be "sick" and that he needs to see a doctor. But the man does not suffer from medical disease neither he suffers from mental illness on the grounds that pedophilia disease is a behavior problem. And the list goes on and on for misdiagnoses of psychologists on problems of living labeled as mental illness.

The misnomer of "mental illness" has continued to serve as a scapegoat of human problems. Financially, it enriches health professionals, psychologists, lawyers, and clients. The tragic result of "mental illness" is the fact that Christians seek help outside the church believing that the pastor or church leaders does not have the knowledge of the cure of problems of living. Believers do not realize that problems of living are spiritual problems, and therefore, only pastors and preachers who are qualified to counsel from God's Word. Spiritual problems are outside the ambit of psychotherapists, therapies, and psychological techniques. It is God who knows exactly the cure for He created the human mind. Thus, problems of living are not mental illnesses but spiritual diseases the cure of which lies in God's hand.

Mental Illness by Ballot

The "mental illness" syndrome has not only spilled over Christians and churches but also spread over the administrator of justice – the Supreme Court, and human association, the American Psychiatric Association. Problems of society such as drug addiction and alcoholism, which were considered before as social problems are now listed mental illnesses by virtue of votes of the U.S. Supreme Court justices. Granting that drug addiction is a social problem he is endangered to receive an infliction of cruel or unusual punishment according to the U.S. Constitution. However, this is too cruel according to the minds of psychologists for a drug addict to suffer infliction of cruel or unusual punishment. Psychologists have to do something to psychologize the judicial system or the bench and convince them that drug addiction is not a social problem or crime but a "mental illness" which requires therapeutic intervention. Convinced by this argument in 1962 the Supreme Court of the United States voted or ruled in favour of the "mental illness" syndrome, and released the perpetrator for psychiatric treatment.

In another case, Powell V. Texas, the Supreme Court was asked to rule the contention that alcoholism is not a crime or social problem but is a mental illness. The court ruled with a 5 to 4 votes in favour of "mental illness." Commenting on this decision, the Director of Alcohol Studies at the University of Iowa, Harold Mulford, said that this court victory is not a scientific triumph but a political one. He stated that science has not proven alcoholism as "mental illness" by definition.

Diseases that are categorized as "mental illness" by psychotherapists, psychologists, or psychiatrists are not listed on grounds of scientific investigation.

"Mental illness" diseases are listed on the basis of the votes or decision of the American Psychiatrists Association. A case in point is homosexuality. Homosexuality has been removed from the list of "mental illness" for the reason that "mental illness" should only apply to individuals who experience conflict about their condition. Conversely, if a homosexual just enjoys or is satisfied being a homosexual he is said to suffer no "mental illness". It is ridiculous to know that the decision to determine whether or not a problem is a disease is delegated to the whims and caprices of the group of health psychologists who are even confused about the true definition of "mental illness." It is sad to know that despite of the presence of scientific technology and medical science particularly at modern times, these pseudo-authorities do continue to be consultants of "mental" diseases that even the terms used in the job are beyond their ability to discern.

The partiality of psychology is becoming obvious. *Caffeinism* is classified as mental illness along with drug addiction and alcoholism. But *child abuse* is a condition "not attributable to mental disorder." Psychic advocates foresee that they need to redefine the definition of mental disorder to correspond changes in the community and psychiatric profession in the future.

56

Personal distress, cultural acceptability, and changing attitudes determine a strange disease known as "mental illness." In the scientific realm a disease is a disease regardless of the circumstances. True, mental illness is a strange disease because it is not even a disease at all.

Disease, Diagnosis and Prognosis

This chapter describes disease, diagnosis, and prognosis in psychology or psychotherapy. The word "disease" only applies to persons who are ill medically. It does not apply to people who are said to have suffered "mental illness" since it is non-existent. To determine the existence of a disease, diagnosis by a doctor or medical practitioner is required so that proper treatment can be administered. Trouble comes when improper or false diagnosis of a person to have suffered with a disease, which is non-existent occurs. Such disease is the so-called "mental illness" as diagnosed by psychiatrists, psychologists, or psychotherapists. With an ulterior motive of collecting huge sums of money, the psychiatrists are hired to diagnose problems of living to be diseases and label them as "mental illness". When problems of living turn to be "mental illness," psychotherapists or psychologists enter the picture since they are the best persons to treat such kinds of diseases. This is where the trouble start for improper diagnosis. They confuse "mental" disease with physical disease. It wastes money from insurance companies, labor, and time.

The term "mental illness" is a confusing and deceptive words, which promote cures for diseases that are non-existent. Psychiatrists, psychologists, or psychotherapists are not the right persons to diagnose this kind of diseases. This role is incumbent on the medical practitioner since diseases fall under medical services. But this is not the case. Psychiatrists do the diagnosis in connivance with lawyers for their financial advantage according to Leonard Kurland. This is fraud perpetrated by lawyers and psychiatrists to defraud insurance companies that problems of living are diseases within the intent of the law.

Diseases that are diagnosed by psychiatrists are absolutely unreliable. Psychiatrists cannot even distinguish between sane and insane person in either criminal or civil cases. They incriminate the person when he is innocent of the crime. This is in violation of the constitutional right of the presumption of innocence of the accused and is contrary to legal jurisprudence. Realizing this phenomenon, in a Texas murder case, the American Psychiatric Association advised the Supreme Court to exclude psychiatrists from trials of criminal cases on the grounds of false expertise that might misled the jurors.

58

Different opinions of psychiatrists from different countries with regards to a disease known as "mental illness" is quite amazing. Each psychiatrist has a different diagnosis of a certain "mental" disease of the same defendant in court cases under prosecution. If "mental illness" is a medical disease then it is a disease irrespective of the person diagnosing it and in whatever country it is located. A chicken pox or appendicitis in America is still the same disease in Australia.

Prognosis is the prediction of the existence of the disease. Psychiatrists are worse in prognosis than diagnosis. They can hardly predict the future behavior of their clients. What psychiatrists do actually when asked in court cases about "mental illness" is to do prognosis on the basis of common sense. The general public, juries and judges do not realize this. The public and the bench believe the findings of psychiatrists are absolute facts. Ronald Schlensky reveals "psychiatrists are no better than other citizens in predicting a human being's conduct." The public, juries, and judges should learn that psychiatrists are not experts in either examining or predicting "mental" diseases concerning human conduct.

The Labeling Game

The labeling game of diseases under the so-called "mental illness" is an unstable task. "Mental illness" recognizes no medical or scientific standard to classify diseases. The label is given according to the taste of the psychiatrist undergoing the diagnosis or prognosis. The following instances demonstrate unscientific bases for labeling certain "mental" diseases.

Firstly, the naming convention of a "mental" disease is subjective. The behavior considered today as abnormal it would be considered normal in the future. A case in point, just a few years ago certain types of hallucinatory experiences would have served as symptoms of "mental illness". Today, it may be labeled as solution where in the past it was labeled as symptoms of "mental" disease.

Secondly, labeling a "mental" disease is culture-bound or class-bound. It means certain types of "mental" diseases only exist in some cultures and classes of society. For example, a black patient may have more "mental" disease than his contemporary white patient. Or, one who comes from a lower class of society may be diagnosed as having "mental" disease as compared to the one who comes from a middle class or upper class. In other words, racial prejudice plays a vital role in the labeling of **mental** diseases whether or not such can be classified as "mental illness."

Thirdly, "mental illness" labeling curtails human freedom. It means that normal people can be robbed of their constitutional freedom at the guise of "mental illness." They will be forced against their will to submit for psychiatric or psychological treatment if they are believed to have mental problems. A classic example, in the Soviet Union, political dissidents were punished and incarcerated in the guise of psychiatric assessment. The dissidents did not go a fair trial but incarcerated until they became fit to stand in court on grounds of mental diseases.

Fourthly, labeling a disease as "mental illness" promotes a self-fulfilling prophecy. It means that if a person is labeled to have "mental" disease such person who is under treatment tends to demonstrate behavior appropriate to the disease he is labeled of. Hence, "mental illness" labeling produces behavior stereotypes.

Fifthly, to label a disease as "mental illness", professionals tend to use words or statements confirming the label. It does not matter whether or not the person under consideration is sane or insane. Once the label is attached, no amount of his denial or defense may be recognized. For example, a research study was conducted regarding a group of sane, normal, stable individuals were admitted as patients in a hospital to determine whether or not the hospital staffs can distinguish between sane or insane people. The result was disturbing because the staffs considered them insane according to the assigned diagnosis.

Sixthly, labeling a disease as "mental illness" excuses or condemns people for unacceptable behavior. If a person's behavior is unacceptable to the psychiatrists, he is labeled to suffer "mental illness." A case in point, a woman was believed to be "negative and disagreeable," one who was very strong of her opinions. She made strong remarks that irritated family members. Psychiatrists diagnosed her to have "organic brain syndrome" – against the testimony of the woman that she was sane and normal. Contrary to witnesses and in spite of the denial and insistence of the woman, she was incarcerated in a ward.

Lastly, "mental illness" labeling frightens people from helping individuals suffering problems of living. No matter how willing a friend or someone to help individual's problems of living, they become repelled and intimidated once the label of "mental illness" is attached to the patient.

Mental Illness of Irresponsibility

This chapter describes human irresponsibility by virtue of "mental illness". Once psychiatrists, psychologists, or psychotherapists label the person to have suffered from "mental" disease they are excusing the person from responsibility of his own actions. This is so because the concept of disease, illness, or sickness in the "mental realm" purports an idea that the person involved is not responsible for his behavior. If he is not responsible for his actions, it is his "mental illness" that could bear the responsibility. So, "mental" disease fabricated by health professionals is used to evade human responsibility. Hence, the psychoanalytic, behavioristic, and humanistic psychological approaches directly or indirectly free individuals from responsibility for their bad behavior.

Psychologists believe forces beyond the control of man do not govern human responsibility. These are called psychoanalytic and behavioristic approaches. The forces that control within the person are known as *psychic forces*. Forces that control outside of the person are known as *environmental forces*. These forces or approaches are so powerful that they render the person involved "mentally ill" and therefore not responsible of his actions. The person involved is reduced to a machine without freedom. To restore this freedom is the exclusive duty of psychotherapists.

The psychological system creates an impression that man is basically "good". The influences of the environment make him evil. Such system robs man of his true condition. He is created and endowed with a will and power of choice. God created him with a power to choose between good and evil. He is responsible whatever his choice is. But psychology removes this power of choice by virtue of "mental illness." It makes him not responsible of his choice.

In criminal cases, the claim of insanity reduces or extinguishes criminal liability or responsibility. To illustrate this point, "diminished capacity" is recognized by the courts of California. In a murder case, Dan White pleaded to "diminished capacity" for murdering San Francisco Mayor George Moscone and Supervisor Harvey Milk. The court sustained the plea and held Dan White cannot be tried for first degree murder. He evaded the heavier penalty for murder and was sentenced on manslaughter charges only. He was released from prison and later committed suicide. By virtue of "mental illness" many criminals are absolved from crimes and hence, instead of reducing social problems, they get worse instead.

Psychotherapy turns offenders into irresponsible victims to evade accountability of their actions. It deals with victim individuals and rarely individuals who are sinners. Psychotherapy sees every person as a victim of one sort or another. It is easy for health professionals to magnify the role of victim.

Human will and human responsibility are inseparable. The power of choice always bears human responsibility. Due to "biological limitations, environmental background, habits established through past choices," degrees of freedom may differ from person to person. God holds each person to be accountable of his actions or behavior since he is given the power of choice. Hence, labeling a person to be "mentally ill" is a direct denial of his God-given ability or power of choice.

Psychotherapy confuses science and "mental illness." The church has been led to believe that problems of living are "mental" diseases. As a result, psychology removes its responsibility for biblical counseling of its members who suffer from problems of living. This is a gross deception since the church or pastor has the proper jurisdiction of dealing with problems of living. Health professionals have no business in interfering the responsibility of biblical counseling.

Is Psychotherapy a Panacea?

The question as to whether or not psychotherapy is a remedy for all problems of living remains in doubt. To answer this question many research studies have been conducted and the overwhelming result is in the negative. Comparing those who did not undergo treatment, Eysenck found "a greater percentage of patients who did not have psychotherapy improved over those who did undergo therapy." This indicates that psychotherapy has no benefit over those without it. In this case, psychotherapy does not work.

Even before the rise of psychotherapy, the improvement rate of those without therapy treatment is about the same today. In his report, Eysenck said that in the 17th century about two-thirds of the patients were discharged as cured. The treatments used to heal these patients were fetters, cold baths, solitary confinement, or extraction of teeth for extreme punishment.

Smith and Glass conducted comprehensive research studies whether or not therapy treatment is better than no treatment at all. The study encouraged psychotherapists since the result would validate their claim. However, the result was devastating because therapy treatment gets mental problems worse.

The theory that psychological counseling works effective on patients remains in question. Garfield admits in spite of increasing research, the outcome does not show strong enough on either psychotherapy is effective or not effective. This is supported by a similar study of Mclean and Hakstian that among the treatments administered on depressed patients psychotherapy was the least effective. Psychiatry professor Donald Klein testified before U.S. Senate Subcommittee on Finance that at present, he believes, scientific evidence for the efficacy of psychotherapy cannot justify public support. And several other research studies show consistent results and do indicate that psychotherapy remains inefficient and ineffective as cure for problems of living.

Self-help and support groups cannot be underestimated. Research shows that self-help and support groups are more beneficial than psychotherapy. It renders a better rate of improvement as compared to therapy treatment. A classic example of this is the Teen Challenge which uses biblical principles, and the Japanese culture. Leonard Syme conducted disease and mortality rate studies throughout the world. The result shows that Japan has the best record of health and longevity due to its close social ties. He believes that the more social ties one has the healthier he is bound to be, and the more isolated a person is the greater possibility for poor health and earlier death.

Since, there exists uncertainty as to the efficiency and effectivity of psychotherapy one has to be warned when seeking for help or cure from problems of living. Often, psychotherapy rather harms patients than cure them. Richard B Stuart said that current psychotherapeutic practices often harm patient they are supposed to help. Other researchers such as Bergin and Lambert claim ample evidence exists that psychotherapy can and does cause harm to a portion of those it is intended to help. Another warning against seeking psychotherapy treatment is that of Carol Travis stating that in a small but significant number of cases, psychotherapy can be harmful and downright dangerous to a client. It appears therefore, anyone who seeks for therapy treatment must be aware of its harmful consequences.

Believing that therapy treatment is all bad is not said in this context. It does not mean just because psychotherapy has harmful effect is bad at all. There are therapists that are good. However, no one knows how many there are who are good. No one knows even if such therapy has harmful or useful effect.

Is Psychotherapy a Palliative?

The belief that psychotherapy does help individuals is the next case to be tackled. Indeed, many do improve without therapy treatment. This brings one to question what factors are involved to get the patient improved.

There is no distinction – psychotherapists and untrained individuals bring improvement to problems of living. People would argue that psychological training would equip one as the best pre-requisite for improvement. This is for the simple reason that psychotherapists are trained in the different methods and techniques of mental therapy. Yet, research demonstrates otherwise. The researcher, Ruth Matarazzo contends that it has never been established that high levels of education and/or training are necessary to the development of an effective psychotherapist. There is no strong evidence to show that there is a relation between the psychotherapist and his training of the methods and techniques in psychological counseling.

Paraprofessionals or non-professionals that help individuals in problems of living are as good as the trained psychologists. It is a shocking observation to hear that non-professionals are even better than the trained therapists. Joseph Durlak states there were no significant differences among helpers in 28 investigations, but paraprofessionals were significantly more effective than professionals. This is corroborated by the interview survey conducted by Bergin and Lambert that the patients were more satisfied from non-mental professionals than from psychiatrists and psychologists. As a matter of fact, those that go to therapy treatment get well due to factors contributed by the non-health professionals. This is what Frank found out that the improvement, which occurred over a long period of time when they were not in therapy, was the result of the effects of this non-professional "treatment."

There is a significant relationship between the helper, not the technique, and the patient in the course of the "treatment." There is strong evidence to suggest that it is the personal qualities of the therapist that help the improvement of the patient. Such qualities as friendliness, conversation, positive attitude, or smile bring improvement to the counselee.

While there are over 250 different approaches that work in psychotherapy, conversation does work, too. In a study conducted by the National Institute of Mental Health shows that talk therapies, warmth, cognitive behavioral and interpersonal therapies are about equally effective. It means that talking to the patient does bring improvement even in the absence of therapeutic methods and techniques. Joseph Wartis insisted, it is self evident that talk can be helpful. This is supported in a similar study by James Pennebaker that conversation is good for the body and soul.

Interpersonal qualities are other factors to be considered in the improvement of "mental illness." It means the interpersonal qualities of the psychotherapist are better than his psychological training. E. Fuller Torry demonstrates certain personal qualities of the therapist – accurate empathy, non-possessive warmth, and genuineness, are of crucial importance in producing psychotherapy. He further notes that therapists who possess these qualities consistently and convincingly get better therapeutic results than those who do not possess them. All researchers, Sloane, Jerome Frank, Bergin, David Hogan, Bryce Nelson, and Jay Haley unanimously hold that it is the interpersonal qualities of the therapist and not his education or training that makes therapy works.

Is Psychotherapy a Placebo?

It is admitted that psychotherapy sometimes as mentioned in the previous chapter is not the psychologist's training that works. Neither methods nor techniques the therapist has done but his interpersonal qualities that work. There is another one besides therapy that works with the person suffering from "mental illness." This is known as the "placebo" effect. Placebo is faith in pill, person, process or procedure. If one has faith in a pill, methods or techniques administered to him, or on the therapists himself, chances are the patient gets well. Conversely, if one has no faith in a pill, person, process or procedure, he will not be healed. The obvious reason why placebo effect works in psychiatry, psychology, or psychotherapy is because it is not science. If psychotherapy is science similar to medicine then whether or not one has faith in the therapy, therapists or surgeon it will work irrespective of circumstances.

Placebo effect is indicated by the following observations and research studies. Eysenck regrets that psychology as science fails to recognize the negative outcome of all studies for the past thirty years to continue using methods that do not present ample evidence to support the claim of placebo effect. If after all psychotherapy works due to placebo effect there is no use for giving health professionals lengthy training in order to practice their skills. The placebo effect of the patient regardless of psychotherapist's training will get him improved anyway. Kroger observes faith and the placebo effect have been over a period of time while there have been variety of new and different therapeutic approaches. He continues saying that the present cure rate for psychogenic entities would not differ appreciably from that of any other period. One reason why psychotherapy works due to placebo effect is because psychotherapy is a state of mind. Thomas Kiernan states that in the end, psychotherapy is a state of mind. If one is convinced that therapy can help him, the likelihood is that it will. If he is convinced of the opposite, the likelihood is that it will not.

Research studies do demonstrate that mental, emotional, and even physical change may occur simply because of expectations. By simply expecting one to get improved it will set the stage for improvement. This is supported by a study on placebo effect which states that it may be that interventions differ in effectiveness because they differently elicit expectancy of benefit. D.A. Shapiro calls it "expectancy arousal hypothesis," saying treatments differ in effectiveness only to the extent that they arouse in clients differing degrees of expectation of benefit.

Expectation of relief works with acupuncture. A research at one university suggests that expectation of relief on the patient influences the result. There is significant reduction of pain when acupuncture is administered in conjunction with procedures designed to enhance subject's expectation for successful treatment. Expectation of relief is the essence of placebo. So, if placebo effect works in acupuncture there is no significant obstacle why it does not work in psychotherapy.

Other researchers reveal that when placebo is at work in the subject's mind, even the false information given to the patient reduces anxiety and stress symptoms. The practice of giving false feedback to the subject is purposely done in Social Influence Therapy – a form of psychotherapy to effect successful result. One practitioner claims that humanitarian fervor aside, it is therapist's job to take power over the patient and convince him he is better, even if it means being devious.

Placebo effect does not only influence the patient but includes those people in contact with him. Each person tends to be influenced that since something is done to the patient then he must get well.

The Emperor's New Clothes

This chapter tries to describe that psychology has paraded all its theoretical embellishments, which are but a cloak of nakedness. Psychological procedures and techniques are just naked theories. They defy scientific investigations. Not only that psychology is pregnant with contradictory statements and approaches which are beyond the limits of science. Psychology has claimed ample unverifiable successes, which cannot be backed by science. These unscientific theories and contradictions are enough to warn people from pursuing psychotherapy treatments.

Christians should not only test psychology if it works but also try to determine whether or not psychology works better than biblical counseling. In doing this psychology is determined whether or not it is more beneficial to the church than biblical counseling.

From the aspect of research psychotherapy has not presented it works better than no therapy treatment at all. Science doubts whether or not psychotherapy really works. Seemingly there exists a logical conclusion that biblical counseling works better than psychotherapy. This is implied from a report by a psychology professor claiming in the first half of nineteenth century at least 70% of patients recovered or improved due to moral treatment to the exclusion of tranquilizers, antidepressants, shock treatment, psychosurgery, psychoanalysis, or any kind of psychotherapy. Due to the myriads of psychological and contradictory theories and techniques, confusing, questionable successes, and unquestionable failures, it is but logical to recommend the patient to refer to biblical counseling. As of today, in spite of the presence of therapists from all walks of life there exists no evidence to demonstrate that psychological counseling is superior to biblical counseling. It appears therefore, biblical counseling can equally achieve with better results for people suffering from anxiety, shyness, marital discord, drug abuse, alcoholism, sexual disorders, depression, and a host of other problems of living. In fact, biblical counseling will do better since problems of living are properly addressed by God's Word.

Christians and the church should not be intimidated of the claim that psychology is superior to biblical counseling. There exists no research studies to support this contention. What psychologists have in mind is to confuse the church so that they can present their gospel of "mental illness", gospel of self, and other religious philosophies. Christians who suffer from problems of living should rather see their church or pastor and not psychological counselors instead.

Christians do not object the use of psychotherapy due to its contradictory theories and techniques, phoney scientific facade, or misnomer of mental illness. Their primary objection is not because the explanation of human behavior is based on the opinions of men and not on science. Basically, Christians do object the use of psychotherapy because it has robbed and displaced biblical counseling among Christians without scientific grounds. Christians should not entertain psychological assumptions but rather hold onto biblical principles. Psychotherapy has no sufficient grounds in overhauling biblical counseling from the list of authorities to the cure of the problems of living. Psychology is a state of mind, a myth, or a hoax in the future. It is rather fiction than fact.

Christians should not be fooled that the continued existence of psychotherapy is not to be construed as an evidence of science. Lots of fake and unscientific theories do continue to exist until today. Every Christian and the church should be warned that the world's insistence in patronizing psychological products does not indicate psychological counseling presents a genuine cure.

Choose You This Day

There is a difference between psychological and biblical counseling although both claims change in the subject's behavior. Psychological counseling is based upon man-made philosophies teaching that man is intrinsically good that there is no God, that man can rise over circumstances and enshrines himself as standard between right and wrong. While biblical counseling depends its cure absolutely on God and His Word – the Scriptures. The Bible calls man-made philosophies, theories, and techniques as "deceptions" that lead mankind to error. God's Word is absolute truth that leads mankind to righteousness.

Man is presented with the following counseling options to effect improvement or change. *Firstly*, that man has to choose either the psychological way or the biblical way. In the psychological way man is a victim. He is not responsible of his problems of living. He has been a victim of circumstances. He sees psychotherapy as the solution. While the Bible teaches he is not a victim of circumstances. He takes responsibility of his behavior and actions. He believes there is God whom he is liable to. He sees the Scriptures as the ultimate and sufficient source for cure of his problems of living. In psychology it is man's opinions that serve as source for healing of his behavior problems.

Biblical counseling is the Bible way of change. Man has to choose the biblical way if he wants healing from problems of living. He has to walk in the Spirit in order to cease walking in the flesh. Walking in the flesh causes problems of living. Walking in the Spirit repels them away.

Secondly, man has to choose either self-effort or faith in God. Self-effort is the choice to do something for his good apart from God. Anything "good" out of self-effort does not last long. For man has no power to do good without God's help. Self-effort cannot perform God's will. But faith in God does. God dwelling in man through the Holy Spirit strengthens man to perform good things. Healing of problems of living that is done through faith in God lasts. Faith in God exercises love and obedience to God. Love for God motivates obedience, and faith in God is the basis for obedience.   Thus, self-effort is not the way of biblical counseling but of psychological counseling.

Thirdly, man has to choose either to do remorse or repentance. Remorse is recognition of wrong but fails to ask forgiveness from God whom he got wronged with. Remorse attempts to pay the price of the wrong done by self-imposed sacrifices, inflicting pains, or flagellations of his body. Remorse is the way of psychological counseling. Repentance is recognition of responsibility for sin. Repentance asks forgiveness from God through faith. Whosoever repents of his sin does not need to do sacrifices, inflicts pains on him, or flagellates himself. A person who repents from sin asks God for forgiveness. He recognizes that sin causes his problems of living. Once his sin is settled he has the power to overcome those problems of living and he will experience long lasting joy.

Lastly, man has to choose either referral or restoration. Referral indicates the Scripture is not adequate to solve problems of living. While restoration indicates repentance, confession, and forgiveness of sin before God through the Bible. Referral is temporary relief while restoration is permanent comfort from God. The biblical way of counseling requires admission of responsibility over sinful actions, repentance of sin, faith in Christ, and a genuine appeal for restoration to fellowship with God. Once sin is settled, relationship to God is restored. Hence, peace and comfort of mind and heart start to dwell in one's life for a lasting experience of joy.

Beyond Counseling

Psychology promotes self-centeredness. It teaches to love self rather than others. It is indicated by constant reference to self, self-esteem, self-fulfillment, and self-actualization. Self is more important than others. The famous psychologist Carl Rogers promotes selfishness and argues it benefits the community or society. The goal of psychology is personal gratification.

Biblical counseling and the Bible promote loving God and others more than the self. The Scripture teaches to deny self. It teaches to love God first, and then others. The last to be considered in rank is the self. Loving others is not an easy task. But, Christ demonstrated it when He came to earth to die to rescue the sinner from sin. He did this because of divine love for sinners. In response, the Christians should not be selfish. They should try to show love, care towards others in the Christian community.

God taught the gospel of love. This was demonstrated by sending His Son to bear the punishment of sin in the sinner's place. Whoever believes in Him is free to love Him and others. Christ puts the believers in the church to express love and care one to another in obedience to His Word. If the Church practices love towards others then biblical counseling has more to offer than the theories and techniques of psychology. The Church is a place to learn to actively love God and others. It is also a place where love from God and others is displayed and received.

Jesus Christ formed the Church from all sorts of personalities, abilities, and weaknesses for the purpose of loving God and others. In this way and through God's Word they will learn to love God, and one to another. Since they are formed from all sorts of characteristics and personalities they will learn to handle and care about different sorts of problems of living.

The community of early Christians was characterized by their common faith, selflessness and their devotion to God, worship, fellowship, and prayer. Because of their faith to God they gathered themselves together to encourage and be encouraged, to learn, to love and be loved, to maintain and strengthen their faith. They were bound to care to each other not only in peace but also in persecution.

The early Christians focused on others and not on self. Material gifts and aids were distributed for the sake of the entire group. They were more concerned on the needs and problems of others than the selfishness of an individual. And above all else, they were devoted to God in obedience to His Word. They listened to exhortation, they preached to others, the conducted prayer meetings and Bible studies from house to house, they were busy caring and supplying the needs of every Christian and lost soul. They worship God together with a singleness of heart and purpose. Everybody was just busy that anyone has no time to listen to the dictates and prejudices of the self.

The cohesiveness of the early church was bound primarily by their absolute devotion to God. They were more concerned on the principles of Scriptures than listen to the philosophies, theories, and traditions of men. They were busy studying the teachings of the apostles. They practiced what the apostles preached and taught them. The early Christians were more concerned in the application of the Scriptures to their lives than the opinions of men. They were busy fellowshipping, loving one another and in prayers.

Until the church takes a dramatic step in devoting to God's Words and forsake all the tentacles of psychology, it cannot detach its affections on psychological counseling. As a matter of fact biblical counseling is not needed when Scriptures is at work in an individual's life.

The True Vine

John 15:1-2 speaks of the vine, which is a living organism of the church that springs from Jesus Christ. Branches that do not bear fruit God the Father does remove them. He prunes those branches that do bear fruit. Pruning by God is needed in many churches who compromise with the world. They need to be pruned in their heart to go back to God. God has to removed those branches that are sold to psychological philosophies, theories, and techniques of the world from the body of Christ. Believers cannot operate in God's love if they do not separate themselves from the world systems.

It is not enough removing the church's psychological ways without the guidance of the Scripture. John 15 outlines three essentials themes for the church to effectively do God's plan. *One*, the church must concentrate its relationship to Jesus. *Two*, the relationship of believers to one another must be in the context of being first of all related to Jesus. And, *three*, the believer must separate itself from the world systems.

The church must concentrate its relationship to Jesus Christ. The relationship to Christ involves absolute dependence on God for everything the church needs. If it has to do anything of lasting value the church must not remove its concentration from Christ by courting psychological opinions. The Church cannot do anything for God without Christ. This is because apart from God all things are nothing.

Since Jesus is the source of believer's life that relationship to Christ must be nurtured and maintained in absolute devotion and obedience to His Word. Abiding in Christ is very significant to any Christian. Living in Him affects the believer's attitudes, thoughts, words, and actions. Concentration on Christ involves all aspects of believer's life. Unless the believer is basically rooted on God's Word, once psychology gains roots through its deceptive tentacles – philosophies, theories, and techniques, it can easily undermine his position before God. To repeal psychological bombardment is difficult outside of Christ.

There is strength in unity. Christians must cement their relationship upon Jesus Christ. Heavy attacks from all forces – evil forces are in operation today. The world is under the dominion of Satan. Christians who live isolated from other believers are vulnerable to satanic deceptions. These forces and deceptions are very subtle that believers do not even realize they are already victims of psychological forces.

Another reason for bonding together in the church is to exercise and learn the expression of loving one another. Unity offers a fertile ground for practicing Christian virtues which are otherwise denied by the world. Loving God and loving one another promotes and fortifies spiritual strength and defence against any attacks of the Devil. By means of teaching and preaching the Scriptures, problems of living are taken care of, hence, there exists a healthy relationship between the believers and God.

Finally, the believer's relationship to God must be separated from the world. The *Compromise Syndrome* of churches today is the language of the day. This is the day where psychological forces and influences against the believer and the church are at play. Unless the church must take its stand boldly in absolutely warding off all tints of psychology from its premises it is difficult to distance itself from the world. The believers should maintain separation from the world to stay pure on God's Word. As a result the world would be hostile to the church but it must be maintained. This is expected because Christians are not of the world.

CHAPTER 3

According to John MacArthur Jr's Book – Ashamed of the Gospel: When the Church Becomes Like the World

Christianity on the Down-Grade

This chapter starts with the famous story of Charles Spurgeon in his downgrade controversy. He separated and resigned himself from the Baptist Union on the grounds that the organization and the church started to preach false doctrines and leaned towards modernism, liberalism, or compromising the Bible with the world. This incident occurred in 1888. But, this is exactly what is happening today. Most Christians and churches do not preach biblical truth anymore. Methods used to gather the lost is no longer biblical. Fundamental doctrines of the Bible are no longer taught. Bible teaching is outmoded, no longer relevant at today's times. Preaching on sin has become offensive. It is already supplanted with various activities such as short talk, film showing, drama, musical rendition, talk shows, and games. Reason for this change from biblical instruction is that people in the church, which is composed of unbelievers, do not welcome any more negative preaching. When in church people want to be entertained and amused.

Lambasting sin and sinner at the pulpit is obsolete and a thing of the past.

Most churches and Christians today adopt the world's strategy of marker-driven policy in bringing people to the church. The church believes business strategies for bringing the lost proves better than following biblical principles. Preachers do water down the biblical message of salvation, sin, hell, heaven, and eternal punishment to suit people's taste. They get rid of confrontational and negative preaching on sin and God. Preachers want the "consumers" feel satisfied and not be displeased with God's Word. When the customer is satisfied it is counted as success.

In contrast, the Bible is uncompromising in its stand on preaching and teaching God's Word. God's Word is relevant to any time throughout the ages. The sinners at the time of Abraham, Christ, Paul, or Spurgeon are still the same sinners that are found today. So, faithful preachers and teachers to the Word should not water down the gospel to accommodate the sinner's taste. Excellent and faithful church ministry is one that preaches the Word – the whole counsel of God irrespective of circumstances. When he charged Timothy in gospel preaching, Apostle Paul said the following statement: *One*, remember your calling. He charges Timothy to preach the Word according to the biblical guidelines and not in accordance to what people like. The faithful teacher must not listen to what the congregation likes but what God requires. *Two*, preach the Word. Paul charged Timothy to preach no other gospel but one that is found in the Bible. He is not to water-down the gospel of Christ. He should preach the Bible as it is to people as they are. *Three*, to be faithful in season and out of season. Timothy has to preach the Scriptures whether or not the audience likes it. After all, he is not accountable to the people but to God. *Four*, reprove, rebuke, and exhort. A preacher should reprove, rebuke, and exhort the sinner to live righteously. Preaching of God's Word should not avoid negatives but a balance of both positive and negative. *Five*, do not compromise. Timothy is warned not to compromise the gospel message at any cost even in difficult times. Even if the church does not like his message he has no option but to preach the truth. *Six*, be sober at all times. Paul charged Timothy to be a stable person, having mortified all his appetites and passions for the cause of Christ. *Seven*, endure hardship. Preaching the truth demands sacrifice of life. Timothy is charged to be prepared to sacrifice his life when preaching God's Word requires it. *Eight,* do the work of an evangelist. Timothy has to reach not only those in the church but also the world of unbelievers. *Nine*, fulfill your ministry. Timothy is charged to whole-heartedly serve God. And *ten*, holding fast the faith. Timothy has to cling, hold faith in God regardless of circumstances.

The User-Friendly Church

Churches of today have changed in worship services and styles from what is clearly biblical. They adopt the market–driven ministry of bringing people as much as they can by catering what the people want and not what God demands from them. These churches are known as "user-friendly" on the grounds that these are customer oriented, customer satisfaction driven, and people's tastes and desires are made the priorities. Some features of these churches are, holding services once or twice during week-days rather than Sunday services. Their messages are characterized with short-talks rather than hard preaching. They avoid preaching on sin and negatives and use palatable words rather than reproving and rebuking the audience with the Scriptures. Pastors and preachers manufacture dramas, plays, films, musicale, and other activities that will amuse the audience. Preaching that pounds on the pulpit is a thing of the past and is obsolete. So the new worship style is characterized as "clever, informal, positive, brief, friendly, never loosen ones necktie."

The contemporary worship styles demonstrate the customer is sovereign. The focus of attention in a market-driven, user-friendly ministry is aimed at catering what the audience want. The pastor must assess what the "felt needs" of the people today. Once he knows this he can adopt strategies or keys that would manufacture ***enormous*** church growth. The "felt needs" to be satisfied with must arise from "issues like loneliness, fear of failure, codependency, poor self-image, depression, anger, resentment, inward-focused inadequacies." Some of these issues are genuine, others are psychological or fabricated. These problems are caused by human depravity or sin. But use-friendly church does not like to address sin for fear of humiliating people or people will not come to church anymore. The contemporary church would rather entertain unbelievers with short talks that would cater their "fleshly" desires and ignore to address their sin for it is distasteful.

Turning the church-growth theory upside down is not an easy task. Sin should be dealt with first before others. Real churches of Jesus Christ are not user-friendly. They preach on sin, hell, heaven, eternal damnation, and biblical principles. The true churches of Christ do address sin and sinners alike. A classic example of this sort is the first church at Jerusalem, the church Christ left immediately after His ascension to Heaven. This church is a huge congregation with tens of thousands of members. Yet, the preachers such as Peter, John and other Apostles reproved, rebuked and exhorted the whole counsel of God to the people. They did not accommodate people's tastes and desires. To illustrate this point, the Jerusalem church agreed to sell their properties and took all the proceeds to the Apostles for administration. One couple, members of the church, sold their properties for the purpose of bringing the proceeds to the Apostles' administration. The couple agreed to bring and give all the proceeds to the Apostles. Ananias and Sapphira as a couple agreed to keep part of the proceeds, and give the remaining part to the Apostles. Peter confronted Ananias that he lied to God when he keeps part of the sale. On the spot, God rendered summary execution against Ananias. Again, when his wife, Sapphira came to the church three hours later, Peter confronted her about the proceeds of the sale of their properties. God rendered summary execution on Sapphira for the same offense committed by her husband Ananias. What Peter did was not palatable to the church or its people. He addressed Ananias' and Sapphira's sin of hypocrisy or lying to God on the spot. Certainly, Peter is not a user-friendly preacher in a non-user-friendly church.

Gimme That Show – Time Religion

With the emergence of the entertainment world the Age of Exposition of God's Word has been replaced and discarded with the Age of Show. Powerful, bombastic, pulpit – pounding, heaven and hell preaching is no longer believed to be a powerful agent of attracting people or unbelievers to Christ. The church adopted strategies from the business world to populate it. Since people tend to assemble in entertainment or talk shows, "show-business" should be utilized to attract audience. Any church that opposes adoption of "show business" strategies is believed to have not fulfilled the Great commission.

The entrance into the church of "show business" strategy did not happen without warning. Spurgeon in his time repeatedly warned in his sermons that hard preaching is becoming obsolete. Tozer warned that people tend to listen and watch shows, dramas, or theatrical performances rather than a straightforward preaching of the Scriptures. Both Spurgeon and Tozer predicted that such situation would occur due to pragmatism in the church. In pragmatism, what the Scripture says is not important, but whatever that works is considered more significant. Preaching on hell or sin is unpalatable and it reduces audience. Confronting people to repent of their sin and turn to Christ does not work anymore. But, entertaining their flesh, covering their sin, telling them they are good and OK is what works. Telling people about Christ, their sin or eternal damnation makes no audience at all.

Pragmatism has been injected into the minds of church leaders today by the market-driven church philosophy. They claim they are successful when their churches continue to add people in hundreds or thousands. When a pastor or preacher leading the church is seen without numerical growth he is despised as unsuccessful and not doing the will of God.

While it is true that genuine leaders or pastors of the church would lead the flock to win the unbelievers, it is their sacred duty to teach or train the flock into maturity and becoming Christ-like. Following men's theories such as pragmatism is wrong and detrimental to believers. The Scriptures and Christ must be the driving force of evangelism and not pragmatism or man-made theories invented by sinful men.   The church is not made for unbelievers to congregate. Christ built the church for the believers' benefit. Below are some points to ponder.

Firstly, the church is not a pub. It is not a place for recruitment of people, entertain audience, a stand-by house of friends. It is not designed to be user-friendly although people who are genuine Christians are friendly not only to believers but also to the enemy.

Secondly, the church is the body of Christ. Church meetings or assemblies are for the purpose of worshipping God and teaching and preaching God's Word. It is not designed to attract unbelievers. Church services are for the benefit of Christians. Christ clearly did not design the church to wait or invite the world to come to its services.

Thirdly, the Church has the sacred duty to proclaim God's Word. The church is not there to stage entertainment such as shows, dramas, film showing, musicale or theatrical performances. It has to preach nothing but the Bible only.

Fourthly, the church has its own strategies embedded in the Bible. It has no business in adopting world strategies and methods to attract people. The market-driven church growth philosophy is a result of bad theology espoused to be biblical. It has its roots from Arminianism. Its main philosophy is that the human will is the decisive factor in salvation and not God's sovereign will. As a result all available human means and methods should be maximized to woo sinners to come to Christ.

All Things to All Men

This chapter starts with the story about Larry Nillsen, a man, who changed himself into a woman through sex-change operation. His name is changed to Sister Paula and became a female Pentecostal televangelist when friends urged her to be one. Sister Paula believes she is more effective in evangelism than one who is a typical "straight" Christian using nothing but the gospel of Christ.

There is no question Sister Paula represents the market-driven church growth philosophy. Her belief is typical to those who hold to this view. The contemporary church must look or behave like the world if it wants to win the world. Whatever the world does it must have its counterpart in the church. Churches now have motorcycle gangs, Christian sports teams, Christian dance clubs, Christian amusement parks, Christian nudist organization, Christian fraternity, and others. Churches must duplicate every aspect of worldly activities or features in order to win them.

The idea of winning the world by doing what it does is taken from Apostle Paul. Its proponents claim that Paul did his best to be like the world when he tried to seek lost souls to be saved. This claim is untenable. Paul did not live like the world when he says in 1 Corinthians 9:19-23, "I have become all things to all men, that I may by all means save some. And I do all things for the sake of the gospel." The reason is obvious. *Firstly*, the gospel of Christ is non-negotiable. By this it means that Paul did not please men or the lost by removing the offense of the cross in the gospel. Apostle Paul argued, "If I were still to please men, I would not be a bond-servant of Christ" (Galatians 1:10). Watering-down the gospel so that it becomes entertaining to the eyes and ears of unbelievers is far from Apostle Paul's conviction that he is crucified with Christ.

Secondly, human rights and privileges give way to the gospel of Christ. If Paul's primary aim is to win sinners, which is the genuine intent of his heart, he has to give up all his rights and privileges in order to win the lost. If in case to talk to slaves, for instance, is not possible without himself becoming a slave, he is ready to sacrifice himself to become a slave. Paul was ready not only to sacrifice and give up all his rights, privileges, and position, but also his life if the gospel requires.

Thirdly, the gospel of Christ does not excuse any Christians to live like the world on grounds of soul winning. Nowhere in Scripture supports that fact. Liberty from the law does not mean that one is free to do what he pleases. What is means, freedom from the law is that Christians are free to do what the Scripture tells them to do. They are free not to do ceremonial rites and activities under the law of Moses and under pagan traditions and rites. Christians are free to live to become Christ-like.

Liberty seasoned with love is the basic principle Apostle Paul had in mind in evangelism. He can sacrifice his human rights, privileges, position, honour, even his life for the sole reason of evangelism. *One*, though Paul has liberty he was a servant of the New Covenant. He was a servant of Christ. As a servant he is willing to abase himself into a status of a salve to win people who are slaves of sin. *Two*, Paul became Jewish to win his fellow Jews. For a Christian who acts like a Jew for the sake of the gospel is meant that he had to adopt Jewish customs. The Jews, contrary to Gentiles tradition, do not eat meat with blood. Paul, in this regard, was ready to sacrifice not to eat meat with blood in order to take the opportunity to preach the gospel to them. And *three*, to the Gentiles, Paul became a Gentile. Contrary to Jewish culture, Gentiles eat any thing with blood including those offered to idols. To Christians, idols have no power at all. Though Paul by birth, he was a Jew, he lived in accordance to Gentiles customs.

The Foolishness of God

Unbelievers throughout the centuries have not always appreciated the reception of God's Word. The attacks have been made always against the truth of the Scripture. There has not been in human history since the time of Apostle Paul that God's Word was free from criticism or opposition launched by secular wisdom. The enemies of God treat the Bible or preaching of the gospel as entirely "foolishness."

However, in 1909-1919 a group of faithful Christians from different denominations all over the world convened an international conference to compile and write articles of their position of the fundamental doctrines of the Bible. This was spearheaded by A.C. Dixon, pastor of Moody Memorial church in Chicago, who later pastored Spurgeon's church – Metropolitan Tabernacle in London. They compiled into 12 books known as "The Fundamentals," hence the rise of "fundamentalism." These Christians believed and defended inerrancy of the Scriptures, its authenticity, authority, verbal inspiration, deity of Christ, substitutionary atonement and other fundamental doctrines of the Bible. However, at the later part of the century, "fundamentalism" has become a derogatory remark, no longer the biblical position of those faithful Christians who founded it.

Nonetheless, *foolishness* is wisdom to those who believe in Christ. Christ Jesus is both the power and the wisdom of God. Only Christians can appreciate the power and wisdom of the gospel primarily because God puts in their hearts divine understanding of the things of God. To expect the world to recognize God's Word as wisdom is not possible and a complete exercise in futility. When God's Word is assessed against human standards it is found to be foolishness. There is nothing to reckon for the unbelieving mind where to base their recognition of divine wisdom. Divine wisdom and human knowledge are incompatible, completely opposite to each other. Any attempt to reconcile the two is certain to produce a watered-down gospel. This is the result of a compromised gospel, making Bible preaching an entertaining one rather than an offensive exploration of the lost soul.

Man's wisdom is inferior to God's wisdom since it cannot comprehend the things of God. God's wisdom is superior since there is no human secrets that God can and does not know. Because man is not able to understand God's truth, derogatory remarks such as *foolishness, simplistic, irrelevant, naive, unsophisticated, obsolete, outmoded* to refer to biblical preaching will constantly be heard from liberals and unbelievers. This is their justification why they adopt worldly standards or strategies to lure people to their churches. They rub out the offense of the cross – the apex of divine wisdom and supplant it with an inferior human wisdom.

It should be noted that divine wisdom is superior to human wisdom for five reasons. *One*, human wisdom is temporary, divine wisdom is eternal. It means that human wisdom changes, contradictory, never solves and makes problems worse. But divine wisdom saves and protects any sinner from eternal destruction. *Two*, human is powerless, divine wisdom is powerful. All the best of human wisdom combined together have never found any solution to the problem of sin. But when one turns to Christ, sin has been addressed and defeated through faith in Christ. *Three*, human wisdom is for the elite, divine wisdom is for all. Human wisdom is only available for those who can afford mentally and materially acquire education. Divine wisdom is available to all who turn to Christ. And *four*, human wisdom exalts man, divine wisdom glorifies God. Human wisdom tries to reach God in man's credit. When the lost sinner turns to Christ, God gives divine wisdom to him and he glorifies God in return.

The Power of God Unto Salvation

Some pastors or preachers believe that different times require different messages. They say that the messages preached by Christ or Apostle Paul 2000 years ago are no longer relevant today. To be effective in attracting the "unchurched" people to listen to the Gospel, its message should be "massaged" to respond the fleshly "felt" needs of today's generation, particularly the "Baby" boomers. Otherwise, the preachers are threatened to have no audience. Massaging the gospel in order to cater the needs of present generation is to get rid of those negative doctrines such as sin, hell, eternal fire, God's wrath, condemnation, punishment, and others in preaching. Besides, the preachers should add humors, anecdotes, games, entertainments, and other activities that beguile the audience to remain listening. Furthermore, preachers should preach in no more than 20 minutes.

The above preaching theory rubs out the essence of gospel preaching. God's Word – the Bible is a timeless sacred document that is applicable at any time, anywhere, and to any individual. There is not a single *message* in the Bible that cannot apply to any person in today's generation. As Apostle Paul asserted, the gospel is "the power of God unto salvation" to any person, saved or lost. It is not the style, the preacher, or the strategies used that makes the sinner turns to Christ.

It is the gospel of Christ that convicts the sinner to turn to Him. To this effect, Apostle Paul has a divine duty to preach the gospel. *Firstly*, he is set apart for the Gospel. Paul stated this clearly in the first verse in his Epistle to the Romans. After he got saved Christ set him apart to preach the gospel to the Gentiles. The gospel is not only for the lost but also for believers. The gospel includes all the revealed truth about Christ. It does not end at conversion. It continues from justification, sanctification, and to glorification. So Paul earnestly preached the gospel not only to the Gentiles but also to his own countrymen – the Jews.

Secondly, Paul served God by preaching the gospel. He counts it not only a duty but a great privilege to preach the gospel to anyone. In this capacity, he did not tone down or ever change his message to accommodate the listeners. He did not worry how people react. He just preached the gospel for it is Christ that turns anyone's heart to trust God.

Thirdly, Paul is a debtor to the lost. Paul's duty to preach the gospel is not because someone has told him to do so but because he is indebted to do the same. What happens if God who is full of mercy did not extend salvation to him? The sure answer is, he would be forever lost. But, due to God's mercy He saved him from sin and now he is indebted to tell others about that mercy of God to any sinner alike.

Fourthly, Paul is eager to preach the gospel. Regardless of the circumstances – whether in prison or outside he had one desire and determination, and that is to preach the gospel. He is unstoppable when it comes to gospel preaching. He is ready to die whatever it costs.

Fifthly, he is not ashamed of the gospel. It does not matter what kind of listeners he had – adult, young, "baby" boomers, man or woman. He was just shameless to preach the gospel. He believes the gospel is the power of God, reveals God's righteousness, and His wrath. The gospel should be preached both the positive and the negative aspect of man's nature. The sinner turns to Christ because of gospel power not on preaching techniques. Hence, different times do not require different message.

Paul on Mar's Hill

Preachers that hold "cultural relevance" is a key to powerful preaching often use as proof-text of Paul's preaching in Athens. Since Apostle Paul mentioned the idols of the people of Athens and his quotation from Greek poets in his preaching it indicates that Paul adjusted, water-down, or adapted his preaching to the people's culture.

This allegation is not true. While Paul was educated not only in his own country but also in the philosophies of Gentiles, he was well versed of the Greek culture, he did not exploit the situation to water down the gospel message. He just preached but Christ alone.

Athens in the ancient world was the hub of intellectuals. In there, the intellectual elite produced sophisticated edifices, work of arts, and philosophies. When Paul visited Athens, he was provoked to preach a powerful message of the one true God. He witnessed to the people of Athens in spite of being intellectuals they were ravaged with paganism and superstition. They admitted a God that they do not know. Paul took this opportunity as the starting point to declare God's Word to them.

Many people heard Paul telling new things. So they invited him to preach to them in the town square. His audience was a mixture of ordinary men, scholars, and philosophers. The philosophers fall into two groups – the Epicureans, and the Stoics. The Epicureans believed that everything happens by chance. There is no God or sovereign that causes things to happen. The Stoics believed everything is god, and everything happens because god wills it. They were characterized as pantheistic fatalists. The Epicureans are equivalent to modern existentialism.

These philosophers mocked and called Paul an "idle babbler" which means seed-picker. To Athens people, Paul is a dull speaker, he does not deserve any attention at all. They considered Paul a fool bringing a weird message to their intellect. Definitely the Greek philosophers were not impressed by Paul's "erudition or cleverness."

In spite of this Paul was so consistent and determined to preach the message no matter what. Anyway, he did not have any survey of this people before he preached the gospel, though. Yet, he did not *massage* the gospel to accommodate the taste of his mixed audience. He did not add any additives to water down the gospel of salvation. Paul's approach, *firstly*, he was polite but confrontive. He recognized of their intellectual achievement to have the capacity to know the "unknown God." But directly he preached on how to know full well the truth about the true God. Paul did not adjust his message for fear of intellectual backlash or rejection. He was bold to declare to the philosophers and scholars that he was going to introduce to them the God that they did not know. In his message he stated God is not unknown but a knowable God. Anyone who wants to know Him must repent of his sins and believe on Him.

Secondly, he related to the philosophers without compromising his message. He described the gods of Athens are man-made and live in man-made temples.

While the true God dwells not in man-made temples. He created all things and is the source of all things.

Thirdly, he was bold and direct. He did not massage his message to suit the occasion or accommodate the tastes of his audience. He preached the gospel message as it is to people as they are. He did not worry about a hostile response, which he experienced later. As expected, the response was contempt, curiosity, and conversion. However, Christians in the secular world may change their preaching style but not the gospel message itself.

The Sovereignty of God in Salvation

On one hand, to some people the doctrine of the sovereignty of God in salvation is a hard doctrine, controversial, unfair, plays favoritism. It makes God unmerciful and does not credit man's good works in salvation. On the other hand, to faithful believers, God's sovereignty in salvation presents God as loving and merciful and man gives all the glory to God. Man is saved on grounds of God's grace and on his works. To him salvation is caused, maintained, and finished by God from beginning to end. Man plays no part in God's saving grace.

It is ridiculous to manufacture additives to massage the gospel to attract sinners to come to Christ for salvation. In matters of salvation any good works on the part of the preacher or sinner has no value at all. No amount of human works can redo or undo God's absolute sovereignty in salvation. Man is saved because God decreed and willed it. No matter how satisfactory man's good works are they are but rubbish and demerits on God's sight. It is only by God's merit through the finished work of His beloved son Jesus Christ that sinner can be saved. If God will not decree that such sinner will be saved, he will not come to Christ at all. In fact, he will get worse because he would just scoff at Christ' sacrificial death for sinners. Conversely, if God will decree in eternity past that a sinner will be saved, such sinner starts to realize he is a sinner, he would humble himself and sees his needs of Christ to wash away his sin. Though he is totally depraved he will be motivated by the Holy Spirit to repent of his sins and come to Christ for salvation.

God's sovereignty in salvation extends to the existence of and His control of all things in the universe. The universe exists as it is now because God has decreed it. All things were created because He decreed it. Every part of the universe functions as it should because He decreed and designed it to be that way.

Ignorance of God's sovereignty in salvation leads to pragmatism in evangelism in contemporary churches. They lose sight of the knowledge that the power of the gospel is the key that unveils hardened sinners. As a result they adopt measures such as market-driven strategies to draw sinners to Christ.

God's sovereignty in salvation demonstrates, *firstly*, salvation is of the Lord. Man is saved not because he desires it but God gives him the ability to desire and appropriate faith in Christ. Man is totally depraved that if left without God's intervention he will never come to Christ for salvation. Pride or good works of man are set aside in Gods sovereignty. Salvation is of the Lord.

Secondly, those who will be saved are chosen by God in eternity past. This election of sinners in timeless past is not due to the fact that God in His foreknowledge saw that they would receive Him or there are good things in them. Under God's sovereignty it is His sole discretion to save any penitent sinner in accordance to the pleasure of His will.

Thirdly, when God chooses people to be saved, He appointed them to sanctification. Sanctification is life set apart for God and live a holy living. God's sovereignty does not cease at salvation. God challenges believers to live a separate life from the world.

Fourthly, believers are ordained to obey God under His sovereignty. This means that Christians have set their priorities to obey Christ and His Word ahead of their personal desires.

God's sovereignty in salvation is not a discouragement to preach the gospel to the lost. As a matter of fact, it will drive every believers to share God's Word to anyone for they do not know who are God's elect.

I Will Build My Church

Proponents of market-driven churches would say they are using business tactics, techniques, or gimmicks, in order to build churches. They believe they cannot build churches at present time without resorting to non-biblical strategies.

But, who builds the Church? The Bible is clear in Matthew 16:18 that it is not the preacher, pastor, or any Christian leader, or even a group or organization. The following describes the characteristic of the church. *One*, the foundation of the church. The Catholics are wrong to ascribe Peter as the founder of the church. The foundation of the church is based on apostolic doctrine and ministry. Jesus Christ is the Chief cornerstone of its foundation. The church is a building of living stones – the Christians whose doctrines are based on apostolic teaching. It is Christ, and not Peter, the Chief cornerstone.

Two, the certainty of the church. The founding of the church is sure to exist. Christ said He will build the church. The certainty of its foundation is guaranteed since it is not based on human resources, strategies, techniques, or gimmicks. It is sure to succeed on the ground that God, not man, is the builder of it.

Three, the intimacy of the church. The Church has a close relationship with Christ. The Church is not anyone's building. It is Christ's.

Four, the invincibility of the church. The church is so powerful that no power or force on earth can defeat its success or existence. Fake churches may come and go but true churches of Christ will persist on earth. Reason, its builder is God and no force can go against Him. Even all the forces of evil are combined, they cannot teardown the church.

Five, the authority of the church. Catholics believed Peter or the Pope has the sole authority to bind or unbind sins on earth. This is patently wrong. When the Bible says that Christ gave the "keys" of the Kingdom of heaven to Peter it does not mean that such authority is only given to him. *Firstly*, the instruction given by Christ is not limited to Peter or the disciples. It applies to every genuine believer.

Secondly, "binding and loosing" does not refer how to handle evil spirits. Christ refers to this as directions on "how to deal with sin in the assembly of the redeemed." Any believer is committed and authorized to expound the gospel message against the problem of sin.

Thirdly, the authority originates from Christ and not from any human being. Christ is the source of "binding and losing" of sin.

Fourthly, the authority is not separate and distinct from the Word of God. God speaks to believers of this authority and this is found in the Scriptures.

The true church that Christ builds has the following marks. *One*, it has godly leadership. The leadership qualities are very significant that it is specifically outlined in 1 Timothy 3:1-7, and Titus 1:5-9. *Two*, the church has biblical goals. Its goals and objectives are not patterned after secular goals. *Three*, it has constant discipleship program to train its members to become like Christ. *Four*, the church has an outreach program to win the lost. Without this constant program the church is doomed to stagnation, decline and failure. *Five*, it has concern for one another. This means that Christians minister one to another. *Six*, there exists a commitment for the support of godly family. *Seven*, there exists solid biblical teaching and preaching of the Word of God. *Eight*, the church has a willingness to change from tradition not at the expense of biblical truth. And *nine*, worship is centered on God and not on human beings. It is not true worship of God if worship is massaged to accommodate others other than God.

Epilogue

Historically, traditional evangelicalism had held to be in the world but not of the world. This stance, however, is no longer the position of the so-called evangelical churches today. Secular influences have been so "powerful, pervasive and appealing" that the solid resistance of the traditional evangelical is already a thing of the past. Biblical evangelicalism has slip into the mire of worldliness.

Believers should be in the world but not of the world. This formula has been reversed by many so-called Christians. This is apparent by allowing mass media gadgets such as cable television, VCRs, radio, computers, and other means of communication to instill in their intellect, and at the same time isolating themselves from personal involvement with the outside world.

Nowadays, it is not the liberal camp that are "modernizers" and compromisers. It is the evangelicals that outdo influences of the liberals of the world. The reason why evangelicals are more modern than liberals, is the fact that liberals came from "evangelical ranks, used evangelical vocabulary, and gained acceptance through relentless appeals for peace and tolerance." This is the kind of tactics modernism does penetrate the fortress of biblical Christianity.

Another subtle approach that can be seen from market-driven mega-churches is their claim that they would never compromise doctrine. They appear to be as orthodox in doctrine while they are unorthodox in methodology. Result, others get attracted with their philosophy and they follow their activities.

The truth of the matter is, doctrinal position to modern evangelicals does not matter to them. Doctrines or biblical principles are not in issue in the market-driven churches. What is important is they can accumulate quite number of people for their church business. Genuine Christianity is not required in modern evangelical ranks.

Bible preaching is a thing of the past. Their messages range from alcoholism, friendship, psychology, self-image, stress management, women's liberalization, homosexuality, and the like. There is no mention of the gospel that convicts a sinner to turn away from sin, encourages holy living, motivates faithfulness for God's service, and warns of God's wrath to unrepentant sinners. The doctrine of hell has been rub off from their Bibles.

In "Christianity Today" an article reports that there exists now a new brand of evangelicalism known as "new model" evangelicalism. Its main features are to redefine Bible doctrines and words. Like for instance, "hell" is no longer to be conceived as a place of torment of unrepentant sinners. It is now a non-punitive place. It is an "exclusive refuge from God's presence, open only to those determined to get there. Sin is another important Bible doctrine that changes its meaning. Sin in biblical sense is enough to put the impenitent sinner in hell to suffer punishment without end. But under the "new model" theology, sin is construed to be a fatherly discipline or correction for a misbehaving child. There is no reason God can invoke sin as a ground for sending any sinner to Hell. And there exists a host of weird doctrines that are redefined to suit their ulterior motives.

If Christians desire to be true disciples of Christ they must solidly oppose this new model of theology and evangelicalism. Otherwise, things are doomed to fail just like what is happening now to liberals and modernists.

CHAPTER 4

According to John MacArthur Jr's Book – Our Sufficiency in Christ

Resurrecting an Old Heresy

A pastor conducted a series of meetings in the churches of North and South Carolina. After his Greenville meetings he went back to his host in Asheville in a cold freezing mid-night. Few meters away from his host, he stopped his driver and sent him home. He walked towards the house of his host hoping that somebody would meet him. However, no one entertained him nor opened the door. He knocked the door several times no one answered. Due to the cold and freezing night he tried to look for a telephone to contact the host. But no telephone was found in the vicinity until he walked farther to a hotel where he woke up the manager. The manager was kind enough to lend him his telephone. He rang up the host. The host told him, he had got the key in his pocket, the host gave it to him before he came here.

This is the common predicament of people even Christians when faced with human crisis. Instead of looking to Christ who is the ultimate key of life, they work by their own way. They try to sacrifice by their own selves to get out of trouble. Christians have the key – "the all-sufficient Christ." They do not need any extra-biblical revelations. What they need is Christ and Him alone.

The denial of insufficient Christ produces gnosticism. This is a philosophy that knowledge of Christ is not enough to supply the needs of the human soul. Hidden knowledge beyond what God has revealed in Scripture is needed for the soul to succeed. Gnosticism existed in the early church. In gnosticism the Bible is not enough. One needs more knowledge to know and satisfy the human needs.

Gnosticism did not only flourish in the past but also there exists a revival at present time. The venom of its influences is very apparent in churches today. The brand of gnosticism is called neo-gnosticism. It is now gaining ground in the churches in the form of psychology, pragmatism, and mysticism.

Firstly, the Christians when in trouble prefer to go to psychologists for counseling rather than to the Bible, pastor, or spiritual church members for sharing Scriptures and prayer. To them God and His Word are not enough to solve their problems. The pastor or any spiritual member of the church is incompetent to deal with the problems of living. Christ is not enough despite of repeated emphasis in the Scripture to the contrary. They believed psychologists are the sole solution to their problem.

Secondly, Christians believed the biblical procedure of inviting sinners to Christ does not work today. Preaching or soul winning should exploit entertainment or advertising that attract the human emotion to get unbelieving audience. Bible teaching is replaced with midweek service. Others have already dropped it altogether. Strong biblical preaching and teaching are replaced with variety of shows, films, dramas, and other forms of entertainment.

Thirdly, not satisfied with psychology, and pragmatism, Christians do indulge in mysticism. Not satisfied with the knowledge of the Scripture and Christ, they seek inner knowledge known as mysticism. Mysticism is beyond the access of human intellect and natural senses. Personal experience is sought rather than knowledge of Scripture. Extra-biblical revelations are better than biblical revelation.

Treasure or Trash

This chapter starts with story of two brothers who inherited the family home and estate. The two brothers did not enjoy with their riches. Instead they accumulated junks – things that are useless. They collected items such as broken machineries, auto parts, boxes, appliances, folding chairs, musical instruments, rags, old newspapers, and assorted adds and ends. All these are rubbish. Both of them shut themselves in their house with these junks. The two died and buried with their collection of rubbish.

This story illustrates a Christian who is sidetracked by the world junks and allurements. Instead to be satisfied with the sufficiency of God's grace, the Christian wants to add more. He has a rich legacy to enjoy given by God. Heavenly and spiritual inheritance is constantly emphasized in the Scriptures. The Christian has been adopted into God's own family. He has all the rights and privileges of family membership, and an inheritance for time and eternity. There is no reason why he desires for more for God's inheritance is beyond compare from worldly treasure.

There are five blessings of God's inheritance. *One*, Christians do inherit God. This is an inheritance which is spiritual. Of the twelve tribes of Israel, it is the tribe of Levi which has no physical or land inheritance.   Their inheritance is God himself. Christians inherit the same. Once they are born again they are born into the family of God. They are God's possession. The Christians do inherit God.

Two, Christians inherit Christ.   When unbelievers get saved they are united with Christ. Christ dwells in their lives and they become His. Christians become Christ's and He becomes their inheritance.

Three, Christians inherit the Holy Spirit. The Holy Spirit is the Guarantor of believers' inheritance. He is the down payment when unbelievers are born again. The Holy Spirit is given as a pledge to secure the believers of the purchased transaction with Christ's blood. Believers' heavenly inheritance is completely secured by God through the Holy Spirit when they became Christians.

Four, believers inherit salvation. When sinners are saved they are rescued and delivered from the sting of sin. Once they are born into the family of God they are forever saved. Nothing can remove them from the inheritance of eternal salvation. Even Satan who is the most powerful force on earth second to God can never disinherit salvation. Eternal salvation is an unconditional gift of God. No curse of the law, sin, death, judgment, or any other forces or factors that is able to disinherit the Christians from the legacy of salvation.

Finally, believers inherit the kingdom. The Kingdom of God is the place where the believers will enjoy once the fullness of time has come. At the moment, Christians are just like "a prince who is too young and immature to understand the favored privileges of his position or the royal inheritance that awaits" them. They may suffer the intrigues and pains of sin but they are not enough to compare with the glory of the inherited glorious Kingdom that is coming to every believer in Christ.

Christians should focus on their eternal inheritance rather than worldly treasures. The Scriptures deal with two revolutionary concepts, which are heavenly mindedness, and delayed gratification. *Heavenly mindedness* is taking off Christians' affection from world attractions but concentrate on God's sufficient provision. *Delayed gratification* is deferring the believers' patience to God's will and God's timing. Its main factor is patience. Eternal satisfaction will be realized in God's terms and not on believers' wishes.

Does God Need a Psychiatrist?

A legal case was filed against Grace Community Church in 1980 for a young man who committed suicide in spite of biblical counseling. The prosecution contended that the church failed and was negligent to refer the suicidal young man to licensed psychotherapists or psychologists. Furthermore the church is not recognized legally to conduct counseling from the Bible where the "illness" falls within the bounds of psychotherapy. Pastors, Bible counselors, and Christians are not authorized to counsel any patient suffering from problems of living. In defense, Grace Community Church argued that the courts have no legal jurisdiction to intervene the business of the church on the grounds of separation of Church and State, and of religious freedom. This means that if the church has fulfilled its responsibility in counseling its members of the problems of living the courts have no jurisdiction over this matter. The Supreme Court of California sustained the argument of the defense. Hence, the case was elevated to the Supreme Court of the United States for review. The highest court refused to hear the case, hence, the ruling of the lower court was upheld.

Christian psychologists are professional therapists rather than biblical counselors. It was observed during the trial of the case above that attitude of Christian psychologists towards the Scriptures is quite appalling. They testified that the Bible alone is not sufficient to solve people's deepest personal and emotional problems. God's Word is not adequate to meet spiritual problems of Christians. What the Christian psychologists had desired is they tried to remove biblical counseling ministry from the church. They claimed only psychologists are qualified to counsel patients that suffer from mental illness. Pastors, biblical counselors, and faithful Christians would feel intimidated in the belief that they are inadequate to counsel Christian problems because they lack psychotherapy training and license.

However one should realize that genuine psychology, which is the study of the soul, falls within the responsibility of Christians and can only be exercised by them. The reason for this is that Christians have the resources and the understanding of the soul according to biblical knowledge. Since psychologists studied from godless theories and assumptions, they are not the proper persons to deal with spiritual problems – the problems of living. Books, theories, training, or techniques do not explain spiritual problems of the heart. It is the Bible, God's Word, that deals comprehensively the needs of the human heart and problems of living. So, psychologists are incompetent to deal with problems of living.

Basically, psychology at modern times no longer deals with the study of the soul. It defines and describes a "diverse menagerie of therapies and theories that are fundamentally humanistic." Psychology is completely incompatible with biblical truth. Christian psychology is an attempt to harmonize the Bible with psychology, a philosophy that leads to failure and is a misnomer since what is really used is godless psychological theories and techniques in the treatment of the patient.

Psychology is unscientific. It is called as pseudo-science. All its theories are human inventions often contradicting which defy the test of scientific investigation. Many psychiatrists do admit this fact. Psychology is based on an atheistic evolutionary theory. Christians who are weak are most vulnerable to psychological deception.

Jesus Christ is sufficient to meet every problem of life. There is no other effective antidote for "mental illness" other than God's Word. Psychology separates the believers from God.

Truth in a World of Theory

"Truth in a World of Theory" describes the truth found only in the Scriptures that cannot be found in the myriads of theories the world has. This truth had been the joy and experience of King David. David had experienced the profound joy and the deepest agony of life. He experienced how painful a son that rebels against his parents, how a son is killed, raped and other tangible life's traumas. But in spite of these worst circumstances, he did not refer to men's theories or opinions, he always consulted the truth – God's Word. He found ultimate joy and satisfaction in the Scriptures. David expressed this joy in Psalm 19:7-14.

One, the Scripture is perfect, converting the soul. By this it means the truth is complete and sufficient. The Scripture is comprehensive in that everything is supplied to the "mentally ill" person. It includes all things necessary for spiritual life.

The effect of God's Word converts or transforms the soul. It transforms the heart. The

Scripture revives and refreshes one's heart. It is the Scripture's truth that convert the heart and soul of the person into the image of Christ. Even the most broken life is converted and restored through salvation into a spirit-filled life.

Two, the Scripture is sure, making wise the simple. In this case "testimony" describes God's Word as a divine witness. "Sure" speaks of the Scriptures as absolute, reliable, unwavering, undisputed, immovable, and indubitably worthy to be trusted. The Scripture is not a collection of theories of men's opinions. They are God's Words.

The Scripture makes one wise. It gives wisdom to any sinner who seeks for it. "Wise" in Scripture does not only refer to facts but includes skills of living a godly life. Anyone who is wise knows the appropriate Scriptural principles as to when to apply them.

Three, the Scripture is right, rejoicing the heart. The word "statutes" refers to precepts. "Precepts are divine principles and guidelines for character and conduct." "Right" speaks simply of what is right as opposed to wrong. The Scriptures indicate and direct anyone from the difficult maze of life to the proper path of living a godly life. Since God's Word keeps believers in the right path, it gives profound joy.

Four, the Scripture is pure, enlightening the eyes. "Commandment" indicates that the Scripture is not a book of options. Neither it is a book of suggestions. God's Word is a divine law that is mandatory, authoritative, and final. Any disobedience to God attracts perpetual consequences. Obedience to God's Word reaps eternal blessing. "Pure" means lucid or clear. The Scripture does not confuse. Neither it is confusing, mystifying, or puzzling. The Bible is a revelation of God's truth. It is not a bewildering book. Its absolute clarity brings one to understanding of its tenets.

Five, the Scripture is clean, enduring forever. The fear of the Lord brings reverential awe before God. It is one that compels anyone to worship God. God's Word is clean, flawless, no impurities, or imperfection. It is not like men's opinions that are full of lies, impurities, or adulterations. The Scripture is permanent, stable, unchanging, and is **relevant to any age and circumstances**. Since it is clean, it endures forever.

Six, the Scripture is true, righteous altogether. In this context, "judgments" refers to divine verdicts from the bench of the Supreme Judge of the universe. This means God's Word is His standard for healing of problems of living and judging the acts and destiny of every person on earth. God's pronouncements in the Bible on any area of knowledge are binding, final and executory.

Psychological Sanctification

John MacArthur received a brochure that advertises hypnosis to clergymen. The advertisement indicates that hypnosis would help develop God-given abilities, live healthier life, and happier lives. Hypnosis is able to resolve conflict by the use of client's mind. It means that problems of living can be solved within the man by exploring himself. Hypnosis answers all human conflicts for the solution lies deep within the inner self. The brochure adds ten testimonies of people that were helped in their hypnotic services.

This is a tragic and worst psychological advice. This is a great lie. There is no answer within the inner self. Man's inner cannot be trusted. Man's heart is bias due to his sin. This is contrary to what the Bible teaches. The human heart is unreliable. It does not even know that psychological theories, techniques or therapies are wrong until he knows God's Word and get converted. An unbelieving heart is a deceitful heart. This is the heart of the psychologist or psychotherapist. Psychologists claim themselves to be the sole qualified counselors of mental problems. Self-examination or psychotherapy is not the solution to problems of living. It is the Bible that has all the sufficient resources to deal for every problem of living.

A letter received by John MacArthur from a 27-year old woman, an unbeliever, tells about a story of the transforming power of God's Word. She was suffering emotional depression since she was 14 years old. She went to see a psychiatrist when she was 20, and had been diagnosed to have a manic depression. The psychiatrist treated her but still suffering from depression. She heard from nowhere that the only solution is to become a Christian. So she decided to listen to the tape messages of MacArthur. She realized she was a sinner, she trusted Christ. She found out that it was sin in her heart that caused her depression. She wrote the only key to heal from depression is obedience to God's Word. She said, "no doctor, no drug can do what the Bible has done for me in changing my life." So, psychiatry or psychotherapy is not the solution since it did not work.

Problems of living cannot be solved by psychology. It is the Scripture that has all the resources sufficient to meet every problem of the human heart. Becoming people of God's Word is a key to a complete cure. Obedience and doing scriptural command makes a difference. One does not need any addition to God's Word. Faithful Christians and spiritual leaders should learn to go back to the Bible and not to psychotherapies.

Christians participate in biblical counseling when they share or instruct one another with God's Word. Even a sick person who suffers from depression can be counseled from the Scripture. A classic example is a dying lady who had terminal illness. She was depressed due to her doubt that although she was a Christian she thought God would not forgive of her sin of cursing God when she got the disease. She was scared of going to Hell. MacArthur counseled and showed her verses of assurance and she was joyful for she got hope of Heaven.

The Holy Spirit has a ministry to believers. Christ told this before He ascended to Heaven. The Holy Spirit fills the human heart with spiritual comfort. When a Christian is obedient to God's Word the Holy Spirit fills his life to be a spirit filled one. Spiritual sanctification is produced by a spirit-filled life. While psychological sanctification is produced by humanistic psychology, spiritual sanctification is produced by the Holy Spirit. The latter is a complete solution to problems of living and a lasting joy to Christians. The former presents no treatment at all for it constantly leads to more suffering of problems living.

Bible Believing Doubters

John MacArthur was invited to preach at Central Baptist in USSR. He observed the church was full of people inside and outside the church. These people were eager and sincere to hear the Word as preached by MacArthur. At the conclusion of his preaching, he invited sinners to come to Christ. The people one-by-one started to come in grief of their sin. Each one publicly confessed repentance from sin and faith in Christ. This was done solely on preaching God's Word only without any aid of "entertainment, no clever techniques, no effort to make salvation easy," and no human manipulation. God's Word is powerful. It does not need any help or additional factor for its completion.

Because the Bible is so powerful, unbelievers, critics, or atheists rally around the Scriptures by challenging its credibility. They question its accuracy, depreciate its precepts, dispute its supernatural character, and others twist its meaning. The worst kind of people that attacks the authority and power of the Bible are those considered to be so-called "Christians." These kinds of "Christians" have been influenced by the wind of the lack of confidence on the sufficiency of the Scriptures. They are Bible-believing doubters of God's Word.

In 1 Timothy 3:16, Apostle Paul lays down four principles showing the sufficiency of the Scriptures for every human need. *Firstly*, the Scripture teaches the Truth. The Bible is "the operational manual of divine truth that must govern" every individual's life. The Scripture prescribes correct antidote for every spiritual problem. One key to avoid spiritual problems is obedience and faithfulness to God's Word.

Secondly, the Scripture reproves sin and error. The Bible gives reproof to disobedient believers. Reproof brings conviction and confession of sin before God. *One*, the Scripture reproves of sinful conduct. Sin must be stopped if one has to recover from spiritual "illness." Reproving with God's Word brings one to realize he is sinning against God. It straightens his life upon preaching the Scriptures. *Two*, the Scripture reproves of wrong teaching. Churches today are invaded with false preachers and teachers. They seduce hundreds of believers away from Christ. Hard preaching against doctrinal errors is a way of reproof to bring them to repentance from erroneous doctrines.

Thirdly, the Scripture corrects behavior. The Bible does not only tell such conduct is wrong and needs to be repented from. It corrects wrong conduct. Any believer who has suffered spiritual problems is brought back to Christ and is corrected of his misconduct. The Bible teaches the correct attitude and behavior. He is cleansed from sin by means of Bible correction.

Fourthly, the Scripture trains in righteousness. Training implies education. The Bible is a great resource of righteous education. Every believer is trained to maturity from the time of conversion. God does not want any Christian to remain just a "body" and stagnant individual. He has to grow in righteousness into the fullness of Christ.

There are two reasons why some Christians claim the Scripture is not sufficient to meet every need of the believer. *One*, they lack discernment of God's Word. The do not study and meditate His Word. The lack of studying God's Word produces meager knowledge of its application. *Two*, lack of pastors or Christians that preach the Scriptures. Many preachers are not real church builders or soul-winners but are Satan's destroyers of Christians and churches. Unless God's Word is preached Christians or unbelievers will continue to claim the Bible is not sufficient to supply every individual's spiritual need.

Religious Hedonism

The power of God's Word is demonstrated when a Jewish medical practitioner turned to Christ by just reading the Book of John. This doctor is an abortionist who appropriated millions of dollars, a divorcee and living with a woman that he does not love. He had a problem that caused him to see a psychiatrist. In spite of therapy his problem persisted. He went to go to church and found John MacArthur. The doctor asked him if he could help him. MacArthur replied he could not but introduced to Someone who knows very well his problem. MacArthur give him the Book of

John and advised to read it and come back once finished. After a week he got saved and his problem was gone.

The Jewish doctor was changed solely by God's Word without any help from anyone or anything. The Book of John was sufficient enough to answer his perplexing problem than any psychotherapy the world can offer. God's Word does not require any methods, strategies, or techniques not recommended by the Scriptures to bring sinners to Christ. The Bible is enough and sufficient for all the needs of sinners.

However, the methods of soul winning advanced by liberals deny the power of God's Word. What they do they manipulate bizarre strategies and techniques to win the lost. Some do exploit secular methods such as "heavy-metal rock, rap, graffiti, break dancing, body building, brick smashing, jazzercise, interpretive dance, and stand-up comedy" in order to evangelize people. Other pastors turned away from preaching to other gimmicks such as drama, film-showing, games, musical extravaganzas, and many others. They believe preaching directly the Word of God is no longer relevant today. Preaching is the thing of the past, and therefore it is outdated. They contend that today's trend needs pragmatic evangelism to satisfy what the audience wants. The following are errors caused by pragmatism. *One*, pragmatism regards methodologies that work as more important than the Scriptures. To the pragmatic pastor it does not matter whether or not the methodology used to attract sinners is relevant to the Scriptures. He caters more on what the "unchurched want", and not what God has commanded him to do. *Two*, pragmatism ignores utterly biblical priorities. To the pragmatist church service is not designed for believers to worship God but catered to unbelievers' needs. Preaching of God's Word is not essential. Church entertainment is better than preaching. *Three*, pragmatism attacks the sufficiency of Scripture. The gospel of salvation is wrapped with human rubbish. God's Word is not required to be told publicly, it should be disguised, "tone it down," or make it palatable to unbelievers. *Four*, pragmatism denies God's sovereignty and exalts human power of decision. Salvation depends on an individual and not on God. A sinner can be saved if he wants to. *Five*, pragmatism reduces preaching to reconciling man to men and not man to God. It is rather man-centered and not God-centered. *Six*, pragmatism reduces the gospel message into little more than a formula of how to live a happy life. Christ can be simply received without obedience to His Word. This is the effect of humanistic philosophy that if people wants to be happy their needs must be met. And *seven*, pragmatism causes apathy about prayer. It creates false independence and self-sufficiency of the individual. Prayers admit dependence on God.

Pragmatists justify their actions from apostle Paul's words that he is "all things to all men." This is wrong interpretation of the Scripture. Paul did not mean one has to live a life of unbelievers in order to win them. What he meant is that he is ready to sacrifice his life at any cost for the sake of winning that lost soul to Christ.

The Quest for Something More

A collector of great works, William Randolph Hearst, one time ordered a piece of an art located overseas. He sent his messengers to buy and to collect the art. But to his amazement, that great work of art was already taken out because it was already stored in his collections. This story illustrates the sufficiency in Christ that a Christian possesses. Some believers seek more additions besides what is provided by God. They do not know that what they are looking for is already in their possession. What is needed is to use and apply the vast and comprehensive resources in Christ embedded in the Scriptures.

Most of the churches are afflicted with material additives that are added to the Bible. They believe God's Word does not provide enough resources for spiritual needs of the believer. They would seek "artificial spiritual additives" such as philosophy, legalism, mysticism, and ascetism.

Firstly, some believers seek Christ plus philosophy. Philosophy is defined as "man's attempt to explain the nature of the universe including phenomena of existence, thought, ethics, behavior, aesthetics, and so on." During New Testament times all attempts to explain God and human beings are classified then as a form of philosophy.

Philosophy tries to explain the human relationship to God. It is required as philosophy claims to understand God and human beings. But Apostle Paul rejects the idea that philosophy is needed to explain man's relationship to God. It is not needed to have faith in Him. Philosophy is wisdom manufactured by unredeemed men. Philosophy is foolishness before God. God never admits man's foolishness. Any philosophy is unacceptable to Him. God's Word – the Bible does not require mixture from man's philosophy to supply man's spiritual needs. The Scripture itself is enough and sufficient for all material and spiritual needs of the believers.

Secondly, Christians seek Christ plus legalism. Legalism involves rules or laws that should be done in addition to scriptural mandates. Some believers believe that observing extra-biblical rules or laws qualify one for spirituality. This is an invasion to the teaching of the Scriptures. Good works, attending church services, prayer meetings, liberality or generosity do not show spirituality at all. These works rather display human pride than spirituality. It is faith in Christ that shows spirituality. Of course, these things mentioned cannot be denied from one who is spiritual. They are spontaneous products of a faithful and sanctified Christian who rests solely on the sufficiency of Christ.

Thirdly, some believers seek Christ plus mysticism. This is the desire of some Christians to display, for instance, "speaking in tongues," as a sign of spirituality. The lack of it is tantamount to not being a Christian. This is again contrary to what the Bible teaches. The Scripture does not admit any other revelation as a sign of being a Christian or spiritual other than what the Bible says.

Fourthly, some Christians seek Christ plus ascetism. This is the belief that extreme personal denial of life's enjoyment results to spirituality. This is not admitted by Scripture. What the Scripture says, one must be born-again in Christ to attain spirituality.

Finally, Christians should seek Christ plus nothing. Christ as revealed in the Scripture is sufficient for all spiritual needs of believers. Believers have all the comprehensive resources of Christ supplied to Christians through His Word. These resources are at man's disposal if done with a right heart and through faith in Christ. He does not need any additives but Christ alone.

A Balance of Faith and Effort

Can a Christian live as free as he pleases? Or, can he live without doing anything for God for it is God who will do all for himself? These questions are found to be the common belief of Christians and churches today. If on one hand the Christian wants to follow God and sets standards for doing or behaving he is labeled as a **legalist**. If on the other hand he wants to obey God by doing nothing and permits God to do all for him he is known as a **quietist**. Now, a legalist is a **pietist**. Expecting God to do all for the individual is *quietism*, and imposing extreme sets of rules to an individual is *pietism*.

Genuine obedience and service to God demands a balance of faith and good works. While it is true that good works do not save a person from Hell, but they do demonstrate that one who is saved from Hell produce good works. Incidentally, neither extreme does demonstrate spirituality. The believer has to maximize his sufficient resources in Christ once he is saved. However, to do good works is not a requisite for the unbeliever to become a Christian. Any good works from an unredeemed heart is unacceptable before God. Without God's love no one can be saved no matter what he does. However, unless the unbeliever is willing to repent of his sins and come to Christ, salvation is impossible. God does not force salvation to anyone against his will. The gift of salvation is God's work. Receiving God's gift of salvation is a human responsibility. This is an apparent balance of faith and work.

God encourages or challenges every believer to live a holy life. Christ has given all the resource so that man can work out his salvation should he choose to obey Him. While the believer is in his struggle in sanctification God is working in Him to make him a holy one.

The believer's divine resources of Christian holy living have five key truths. *One*, His Person is God. Spiritual progress of every believer is not reckoned from his abilities to do good works but from God. When a Christian is willing to do God's Word, obey His will, live a holy life, God strengthens him in order to do good works. God has the power to change his sinful life into a brilliant and godly one. He may stumble into sin but Christ's sufficiency is able to lift him up and continue walking on the road to sanctification. He cannot live a holy life without God's empowerment.

Two, His power at work. It is God's power that energizes the believer's life to sanctification. God's power at work compels him to live righteously, hates sin, be diligent and obedient to God, and apply scriptural principles.

Three, His presence in the believers. Christians are privileged group of people. God the Holy Spirit is always present in the believer's life. Since He is always there He is grieve when he commits sin. He indwells the believer from the time of conversion. That is why, it is not impossible to live a sanctified life because God is always there to give help.

Four, His purpose is to will and to work. The believer works toward his sanctification. This is done by God energizing his will or desires to do good works or deeds. *Firstly*, God puts the Christian holy discontent to his human flesh and desires. *Secondly*, God makes his desires to conform to God's aspiration.

Five, His pleasure is God's good pleasure. Man was created for a purpose. God created man to give pleasure to Him. The Christian is saved to give glory to God. The believers are very precious to Him. Christ died for them for purposes of God's pleasure. God is glorified when Christians live a holy living.

Spiritual Warfare: Who After Whom?

Some Christians are led to believe and even practice "spiritual warfare" in the belief that Satan could be stopped from harming people. There are groups of so-called "Christians" who practice exorcism to rebuke or bind Satan and other demonic forces. While it is true that this world is under the influence of demonic forces led by Satan, he is a defeated foe or power. This is included in the sufficiency in Christ that every Christian can be victorious over the Devil. The practice or art of studying "techniques for confronting and commanding evil forces, binding" the devil, "breaking the strongholds' of territorial demons, and complex stratagems of meta physical combat" does not work. It is God's Word that has the power to bind or rebuke Satan. The practice of developing strategies and techniques as tools to combat in "spiritual warfare with the Devil has already penetrated church fortresses. Some believers believe that one need to be able to rebuke Satan to stop him from harming evil. This is a wrong doctrine which springs from mysticism. The church should stand on the sufficiency of Christ and His Word to confront demonic powers. The reason why believers should not practice strategies or techniques other than the Scriptures against Satan is clearly outlined in the Bible. *Firstly*, the believer has no power to rebuke Satan. Even the most powerful angel – Michael himself did not rebuke Satan. When Satan disputed the body of Moses, Michael told him God rebukes him. *Secondly*, Satan is a defeated enemy. Rebuke is a strong action which only God can use against Satan. By simple resistance against satanic forces through faith in Christ will work.

The fact that Satan is a defeated enemy, it does not mean he has no power to temp or harm believers. Every Christian must know that Satan tries hard to catch victims from children of God. His main target is to destroy God's work and the believers. Any believer is his target by taking him away from God's hand if possible.

Likewise believers should know that no amount of Satan's temptation through inflicting pains or sufferings would work without God's permission. A classic example of this is Job. Satan, without Job's knowledge was permitted by God to inflict pain and suffering. God has the best knowledge why He permitted him. What is found in Scripture is that Job's experience brought glory to God's name.

There are two major strategies Satan has used against God's people. *One*, Satan blinds the unbelievers. He takes away the wisdom to understand God's Word, robs the joy of salvation, removes the reality of Hell and the consequences for having no Christ. He influences people to scoff at the gospel of Christ, instill skepticism about the truth, and puts delusion on people's minds that Christians are the ones who are satanic forces.

Two, Satan tempts believers. Not satisfied with just blinding the unbelievers, he attacks Christians through temptation to lead them to sin. He keeps things very attractive to Christians in order to lure their focus away from Christ.

Thirdly, Satan is used sometimes for God's glory. Although, some believers may not admit this fact, there are instances Satan's role in believer's life brings God the glory. A classic example is Paul who suffered a "thorn in the flesh" in his entire life inflicted by Satan. Apostle Paul understood this why God allowed Satan to buffet him. The reason is prevention of pride so that Paul may not develop it in his stand for Christ. Another example is, delivering backsliding Christians to Satan for the prevention of further damage of the gospel of Christ and harming the testimony of God's people. This is to prevent them from hindering the influence of the gospel from people's lives.

Sufficient Grace

This chapter starts with a story of a poor young man who had sacrificed and saved every penny to attain his dream to go on a cruise once in his life. He was able to attain his dream but while he was on luxury cruise he only ate bread and peanut butter while other passengers enjoyed luxury food. Feeling hungry, one day he approached the porter who was in charged of taking passenger's orders and asked the price for ordering the food. The porter told him that if he has the ticket for the cruise, the food is free. Then, he ordered the luxury menu. Many Christians are just like that poor young man. They do not realize that all their needs have been already provided when they became born-again believers. God's resources are comprehensive and sufficient to supply every need of the believers. Every believer is saved by grace. Grace upholds man's salvation, gives him victory over temptation, helps endure pain and suffering, brings understanding of God's Word and its application. It draws believers into communion and prayer. Grace enables believers to serve God effectively. Christians do live in an environment of all-sufficient grace.

God's grace is characterized by *firstly*, grace upon grace. This is the grace which accumulates one upon another. *Secondly*, super-abounding grace. Every believer is guaranteed with the supply of grace that extends no bounds. And *thirdly*, all-sufficient grace. This is the grace that endures hardships.

The grace of God teaches believers the great lessons of life. *One*, it teaches humility. Through suffering, the Christian is taught how to abase himself. Pride is inherent in anyone's life. Without God's grace it is difficult to take away pride. Christians do have pride particularly when they are in positions of spiritual grandeur. But, through grace, every Christian is made humble since they do not get the credit. It is God who should get the credit. When God sees that the believer has already "puff up" He brings opposition and sufferings to remove his pride.

Two, grace teaches dependence. For believers they get all their resources from God. Without God's sufficient grace they are nothing. Paul learned dependence on God when he asked Him three times to remove his "thorn in the flesh." God taught him grace of dependence by denying Paul's desire.

Three, grace teaches sufficiency. Denying Paul's desire, God guaranteed him that His grace is sufficient to sustain his pain and suffering due to His "thorn in the flesh." Believers depend on God for supplies of spiritual needs. But, not all things are granted since they asked for it in their own terms and not according to God's will. God's answer is sometime, "NO" to display his grace of sufficiency.

Four, grace teaches power. Though Christians are weak God strengthens them. God's strength is only bestowed when the believer is weak. They are enabled to stand for the truth through the power of the Holy Spirit.

Five, Grace teaches contentment. There is no contentment in the world. But through grace, God brings satisfaction and blessing far and beyond what the world can offer.

Trials and sufferings are God's tools to show His sufficient grace for the maturity and purity of the believers. Trusting on God's sovereign grace removes fear, anxiety, and worry when things go wrong. Because of God's abounding grace the believer is able to stand against sufferings. For the Christian, sufferings verify the strength of his faith. It tests whether or not his faith stands amidst fire of sufferings. Not only that suffering confirms sonship of God, it also produces endurance, teaches to hate sin, promotes self-evaluation, clarifies priorities, identifies with Christ, encourages other believers, benefits unbelievers, and enables to help others.

Epilogue: Perfect Sufficiency

Human wisdom cannot provide resources for the needs of believers. Resources that are sufficient enough to supply Christians spring from God. Human books cannot deal with spiritual matters. These spiritual resources cannot be obtained anywhere other than from the revealed Truth of God – His Word, the Bible.

One of God's names means "the All-Sufficient One." This is taken from His name "El Shaddai." It means that the believer's need can only be satisfied by

God for He possesses all the resources he needs. God is the only adequate resource of the necessities of life. The believer does not "need any supplementary experience, a stronger dose of His redemption, or any other spiritual or emotional accoutrements." He does not need any therapeutic or psychological additives to satisfy his life's needs. Once he is saved the Christian has all the abundant resources ready for use. These resources accomplish his deepest desires to enjoy life, and to be spiritually righteous. He does not need to go to any religion to obtain spiritual happiness. He does not need to practice mysticism, or join organization to acquire satisfaction. What he needs is God. Secular materials do no offer lasting genuine joy. Material resources just only bring to believers more miseries. But, through obedience and searching of God's Word, the believer will be able to find spiritual satisfaction far beyond the world can offer. God is enough for every human and spiritual longings of the believer.

Few books describe God as generous. Perhaps, theologians spends lots of time arguing who God is to the extent that they forget to write and learn that the great Creator of the universe is very generous. His generosity was demonstrated when God sent His only begotten Son, left His throne in glory just to die for sinful human beings from sin. Now, if the Father did not withhold His Son to die for ugly, unworthy, undeserving sinners, will He not give all the needs and longings of believers including cure for problems of living and enjoy them in their lives? If God the Father could afford to give His only Son as a supreme Gift of sinful men, can He not supply and give all His resources for sinners to enjoy? The certain answer for these queries is a resounding affirmative response. God will not withhold any spiritual resources to be enjoyed by His children according to the pleasure of His will. Christ whose riches are exceedingly abundant is adequately sufficient to supply every necessity of life. God's sufficiency is absolute. His sufficiency never diminishes. It is only man that is in short of faith in God that he does not enjoy God's sufficiency. Lack of sufficient spiritual resources may be caused by utter disregard of God's Word, living a wicked life, or perhaps, his heart is not regenerated. However, once the Christian is obedient, challenged to know God better, serve Him faithfully, live to be more like Christ, His absolute sufficiency is for him. That is why Christians need to be challenged to serve Him in the sincerity of His heart.

Instead to be burdened with trials, sorrows, and discouragements, why not Christians obey God and maximize His sufficient resources? Life's difficulties cannot be solved through secular resources but through God's spiritual resources.

CHAPTER 5

According to John MacArthur Jr's book – The Vanishing Conscience: Drawing the Line in a No-fault, Guilt-free World

Whatever Happened to Sin?

In today's society guilt, like sin, is no longer called as it is. Criminals and murderers are told they are not responsible for what they have done. They are just victims of circumstances. Psychologists tell them to refuse "guilt" feelings within themselves. Society may allow and encourage sin but will not tolerate guilt. Therapists described guilt as not conducive to human dignity and self-esteem. Wayne Dyer describes guilt as "the most useless of all erroneous zone behaviors." He further said guilt must be completely cut-off, "spray-cleaned and sterilized forever."

To completely cut-off guilt is to defy or fight against one's guilt. Every person or relative who blames him for his sin must be stopped from blaming his guilt. Any semblance of guilt in one's emotion must be refused if one wishes to be released from it. Any attempt for personal responsibility must be refused and denied to avoid guilt.

The reason why guilt should not be allowed to take hold on one's emotion is because it has the power to take all the joy of life. So, psychotherapists try to advice: "stop being tough on oneself, admission of guilt drives one crazy, get rid of the guilts, stop pleading guilty, do not feed the guilt-monster," and other words of similar import. Ignoring blame or guilt is one of the best formula to treat one's self from guilt. Claiming not to be at fault for one's misbehavior is a good therapeutic advice for guilt-spray cleaning.

"Victimism" is a word that describes the kind of morality that a society possesses today. Instead of admitting sinners to be guilty, criminals or murderers, or people who misbehave themselves are just encouraged to claim they are victims of the circumstances. People who murder others could claim themselves as victims of what they have done to excuse criminal liability. They do not claim responsibility of their actions at all. Criminals escape punishment because they are not guilty since they are just victims of circumstances.

Escaping blame or responsibility is a result of the "sin-as-disease" model perpetrated by psychologists. There is no such thing as sin of drinking intoxicating liquors, sin of drug addiction, sexual sin, and others. These are just diseases like those classified as medical diseases. Children who defy parental authority are said to be suffering from hyperactive illness and not to be considered as disobedient children.

A parent who shuns family responsibility and uses his money to indulge in sex with prostitutes is not sin or said to be responsible of his family since he suffers from sex addiction disease. What he needs is treatment from therapies instead of punishment.

The effect of sin-as-disease model gets worse. There is an ever increasing number of victims dependent on therapies. This is a clear indication that psychotherapists are no solution to the sin-as-disease illnesses. This model has been made as a scapegoat for accumulating millions of dollars in the therapy industry. Clearly, psychology is not a solution to the problems of behavior.

The sin-as-disease model does not only infiltrate society but it has invaded the church. Church leaders have been "psychologized" that if a member suffers from one of its diseases they immediately call or refer him to therapies rather than to God's Word. Guilt or sin is hardly identified as sin or evil and that it no longer requires the antidote of God's Word. Denial of guilt or sin is an exercise in futility. It does not address the problem. But acceptance of the responsibility of sin or guilt does.

The Soul's Automatic Warning System

This chapter starts with a classic story of an airplane that crashed because the pilot ignored and switched off its automatic warning system. All the people on board died. It was only the "black box" cockpit recorders that revealed the real cause of the accident.

Conscience is like the airplane's automatic warning system. It can be switched on or off depending on the discretion of the person concerned. Human conscience warns the person before it crashes and burns. It tells him he is wrong or he is right. Good conscience encourages or entreats one to do what he believes is right. It restrains or prohibits one from doing wrong when he believes it is wrong. Conscience judges one's actions and behaviors on the basis of the highest standard he perceives. It condemns when conscience is violated resulting in emotional depressions, feelings of shame, anguish, regret, worry, and others. When conscience is followed, it commends one resulting in joy, peace, self-respect, well-being and gladness.

Most people react to their automatic warning system negatively. Instead of listening to its warning of disasters or failures, they ignore it, switch it off or suppress it. Through the effect of psychology man's conscience is turned off. To claim that alcoholism, sexual indulgence, immorality, committing crimes and other vices are not sin but just "mental" diseases is an indication that one's conscience is down or switched off.

If conscience is not suppressed it functions properly and is a better witness to oneself. It knows every secrets of the human heart. Conscience tells the truth regardless what one or others would say.

However, conscience can be switched off. It does not react to any activities of the human being. It does not give warning about what is happening or consequences of one's actions. When this is the case it is a sure indication of a forthcoming disaster of one's life. This kind of conscience is found in psychopaths, serial killers, pathological liars, and persons whose consciences are no longer sensitive to the call of what is right or wrong.

Conscience acts like a court in the judgment bar of the human heart. It is a register recording the precise details of what is happening in one's heart. It accuses him if he is guilty, and defends him when he is innocent or right. It is a witness for or against him. It executes him through grief when he is discovered.

Conscience is rejuvenated or is back to life when it is cleansed by the blood of Christ. This happens at salvation when someone realizes he is a sinner, in humility he repents of his sin, and come to Christ through faith.

In a Christian environment there is a strong and a weak conscience. Strong conscience is one that is tampered and has matured through God's Word. Weak conscience is one who has not matured in God's Word and is a babe in Christ. Christians with strong conscience should be careful to damage the weak conscience.

A pure conscience can be obtained through confession, forgiveness, restitution, instant action, and education. To have a pure conscience one must confess and admit his sin. He must ask forgiveness of his sin from God. He must pay for whatever he has damaged. He should deal at once when conscience is violated. And, one must educate his conscience with the standard revealed in the Scriptures. A pure conscience should be the clothing of every spiritually matured Christian. It should be desired and possessed without seeking approval from the world.

How Sin Silences the Conscience

A conscience that is soaked with the toxins of sin does not react anymore for goodness. It is seared, it no longer has the power to recognize between right and wrong. When people begin to claim irresponsibility or start claiming they are victims of what they have done it is certainly an indication that their consciences are dead.

A dead conscience is a result of a hardened heart by the deceitfulness of sin. Today's society is characterized by a dead conscience. Sin erodes the human heart and society. Sin causes the human heart and society to slide down to destruction. A dead conscience is not disturbed by sexual perversion, gross immorality, or criminal propensity. What was considered before as taboo and immoral it is now fine and good in today's society. A classic example of this is the "Phil Donahue" TV show. People who are displayed there are very frank and absolutely seared of speaking gross immorality. They have the guts to speak crimes and activities which before were not even seen in public. Its audience give more praises of approval to those who can speak more grisly immoralities.

The homosexual epidemic is flooding the streets of urban cities. Homosexuality is condemned as evil by the Word of God. But in today's society, politics, religions, and humanism salute with loud praises towards gay and lesbian activities. When government authorities are confronted they argue for understanding and tolerance towards homosexuals. As a result, gay and lesbian activists do continue to press their demand for public recognition that homosexuality is not wrong. It is a sexual alternative to heterosexuality.

In Romans chapter 1, homosexuality is judged as absolutely evil. God did not legislate an alternative option to heterosexuality.   Since homosexual practitioners do insist continuously in their sin God gave them up removing their conscience and their automatic warning system between right and wrong does not work anymore. Because homosexuality is a gross immorality there can be no easy solution not until they would admit and turn away from their sin and come to Christ.   There is no known technique for conscience restoration outside of Christ.

The downward motion of today's society is characterized by the following factors. *One*, foolish speculations. What this means is suppressing the truth or God's Word. To suppress truth is to ignore or reject God's Word in one's life. Rejecting any semblance of God in man's life results in silencing human conscience.

Two, death of common sense. To refuse to honor God indicates lack of understanding, and that shows death to common sense. Teaching people there is no God, the Bible should not be taught in school, or animals are accorded human rights rather than human beings demonstrate a ruined logic of common understanding.

Three, corrupt religion. Illegitimate and corrupt religion indicates idolatry by worshipping anything other than God. Corrupt religion results in a corrupt immorality. Introduction of humanistic psychology, witchcraft, occultism, cults, satanic worship or new age movement, does anesthetize the human automatic warning system – the conscience. Today's society worships the environment, dolphins, animals, Mother Earth, more than God.

Four, uncontrolled lust. Lust refers to sinful desires which include insatiable hunger for pleasure, wealth, power, prestige, and sex.

Five, sexual perversion. It includes homosexuality, pedophilia, sadomasochism, necrophilia, or bestiality. Due to society's moral decadence, God has removed His restraining grace to prevent one from doing evil. When God's grace is wanting, human conscience is dead.

What Do You Mean "Totally Depraved"?

Psychologists believe that making people feel good would solve all problems of living. Self-esteem is the teaching that problems of living can be solved through making people feel good. The reason why crimes are committed is because people have no enough self-esteem. The lack of it breeds lawlessness, immorality, violence, and wickedness. There is no distinction whether self-esteem is at its low level or the lack of it, wickedness of humanity would result. If a child or student is disrespectful to his parents or teachers it is because he lacks or has no self-esteem. Conversely, if he has self-esteem, he shows respectful behavior and therefore not a menace to society.

Does self-esteem really work as a panacea of human problems? The answer is absolutely in the negative. One classic example illustrates this better. A standardized maths test with a question whether an examinee is good at maths or not was conducted to students coming from six nations. The result is devastating. The American students whose daily menu is self-esteem scored lowest with their affirmative answers that they are good at maths. While the Koreans scored at the top without help of self-esteem with their resounding negative answers that they are not good at maths.

The sting of self-esteem theology does not only infect the secular world but has already traversed the portals of churches and Christianity. A noted evangelical clergyman of "Positive Thinking", Norman Vincent Peale popularized self-esteem doctrine. He writes a book on positive thinking with notes stating self-esteem is "applied Christianity". His ideas of self-esteem reaches his disciple Robert Schuller who wedded self-esteem and theology. Robert Schuller's doctrine is completely opposite of what the Bible teaches. He says that man should not be taught that he is a sinner for it offends him. Human beings should be glorified. He believes sin is a psychological self-abuse. Schuller does not believe self-esteem indicates total depravity of man. He claims all human beings are essentially good. There is no such thing as evil person.

However, the Bible teaches otherwise. In fact, the Bible approaches man as essentially evil. Salvation is never possible not until the sinner is told he is a sinner; he should admit that he is, and he needs a Savior – Christ Jesus. Clearly, the Scripture teaches against self-esteem. It teaches total depravity of man. Apostle Paul outlined human depravity in the early chapters of Romans. *Firstly*, Paul charges that all humanity is under sin. This means that there is no single person on the face of the earth that is not a sinner. Each individual is totally depraved.

Secondly, Paul present proofs that man is totally depraved. *One*, he says sin corrupts character. Of all the millions of people in the world there is not a single one found to be righteous. *Two*, sin defiles conversation. The behavior of the person is known by the way he speaks. No one speaks righteously. Total depravity is universal. Wickedness is found in every society. *Three*, sin perverts human conduct. This means total depravity is demonstrated when people commit crimes without regard of God and human law. People kill others even without reason at all.

Thirdly, Paul concludes his verdict. Since each person on earth does wickedness, each of them is guilty of sin before God. All sinners are guilty before God. There is no ground for acquittal. However, God offers one chance to turn away from sin and come to Christ through faith. Repentance and faith towards the Lord Jesus Christ is the only biblical basis of justification. Self-esteem never works for it is wanting of God's mercy.

Sin and Its Cure

Man is naturally a fallen human being, his tendency to sin rather than righteousness demonstrates his total depravity. Man loves sin so much that he cannot do anything without it. Without God's intervention of grace, there is nothing that bars him from eternal condemnation in hell.

Sin has never been a human benefit. When sin enters the human heart it rules over his life. It has an addictive effect that once it is allowed entry in the heart there is no turning back. Sin not only rules his life but it destroys God's human creation, stains the soul, degrades his nobility, darkens his mind, makes him more worse than the beast. Sin is all disgusting, loathsome, and revolting before God. The consequences of sin terribly attract the eternal punishment in Hell of which without God's intervention of grace, all people without exception are already heading there.

Sin is not a weakness or disease that would release one from responsibility. Man fell into sin by choice. Had he chosen not to commit sin, he would have lived righteously until today without any problems of living. When Adam sinned he knew he did it. The same is true to all people today they are not innocent of what they do. But instead of admitting sin before God, Adam did the following actions. *One*, he tried to cover up. When man knew he sinned against God, he provided "fig leaves" of righteousness for covering of his sin. He believes if he does this God would not see what he has done.

Two, he attempted to justify himself. When God confronted Adam why he did violate God's instruction or law, he replied he is not at fault. God has to be blamed and not Adam because He made Eve for him to commit sin. People of today is no different from Adam. When one kills another person, the perpetrator always denies he did the killing. It is someone else's fault. Sin always looks for scapegoats to avoid responsibility.

Three, he is oblivious to his own sin. This is committing sin in ignorance or presumption. A person may admit he did sin but it was done because he did not know it is sin. Or, he presumes God will understand him because he is just a human being who is subject to commit errors.

There are many attempts to explain the problem of sin which is known as "Theodicy". *Firstly*, man flatly denies the existence of evil. This is absolute denial that there is no bad thing in the world. Evils, diseases, negative effects or calamities are simply figments of imagination.

Secondly, God is powerless to control human choices. He has no command over circumstances in the universe. God is also a victim of sin. However, this view is faulty. God is sovereign over His creation and circumstances. He is always in control from eternity.

Thirdly, God permitted the entrance of sin into the world. Sin did not enter the world without God's knowledge. He planned, and decreed it in eternity according to the pleasure of His will. He uses sin to accomplish His purposes and for His glory.

Since every person in this world is a sinner, his sin cannot improve his condition without God's assistance. He will only get worse. Sin has no power to improve itself. No amount of human goodness, prayers, sacrifices, love, kindness, or evilness that can ever save a person from sin. Turning away from sin and coming to God in faith is what makes the sinner saved from sin and it avoids terrible consequences. The element of repentance and faith are indispensable requisites for the sinner's healing from sin. Repentance itself does not save. Faith in Christ does.

The Conquered Enemy Within

Man sometimes invoke imperfection to justify his sin. The phrase "nobody's perfect" reverberates in almost anyone's mouth to include Christians to feel himself better. So, there is no reason why man cannot stop sinning because he is just a "human being", prone to commit errors. Imperfection has become an excuse to commit sin instead of not doing wrong.

The Scripture teaches man is not perfect. Man is just a human being who is capable of sanctification.

The Bible never allows imperfection to be a ground for justification over sin. Perfection over sin cannot be obtained during this life. Since perfection against the flesh is impossible while man lives, sanctification has to be applied in Christian's everyday living.

Perfectionism is wrongly interpreted by individuals or organizations. A classic example of this is the Oneida Community, which occurred from 1849 to 1879 in New York led by one John Humphrey Noyes. He founded this community in the belief that perfectionism is attained during life. However, the facts gathered from this community is quite bizarre to human standard of morality. Any man can have sex with any woman in the community. The founder himself had to deflower the young girls as soon as they reach pubertal stage. And there are lots of other examples. Another type of perfectionism is the "Holiness" movement which has its root from Wesleyan theology. It includes traditional Methodism, Salvation Army, Church of the Nazarene, and many charismatic denominations. This type of perfectionism believes that sanctification is done at once through a second work of grace. It teaches that sanctification or perfection occurs as a second work of grace or second blessing separate and distinct from salvation.

These perfectionist movements actually have a sub-standard morality. Sin is redefined according to their taste. Human failures are called "mistakes" or "temptations." They are not called sins. Evil doings describes in Scripture are first known as misdemeanors.

Perfectionism is a gross interpretation of sanctification described in the Bible. Sanctification is not a "one-act" operation. It is a process. It starts from conversion up to the time of glorification. Sanctification is God's work in the believer's life from the time God saved him from sin until he becomes a glorified body. Sanctification takes time, requires the constant guidance of the Holy Spirit through God's Word in the believer's life. It is unattainable in life. Every Christian is set apart to be Christ-like but he can never be perfect while he is alive. The reason why perfection is unattainable during life is because the Christian is saved from sin, he has still the influence of sin in his life. The principle of the flesh still clings to him. This is not eradicated at conversion neither at sanctification. The flesh is only absolutely removed when the Christian is finally glorified. All movements of perfectionism are just attempts of and disastrous misunderstanding of the doctrine of sanctification of the Scriptures.

However, imperfectionism cannot be invoked as ground for continuance in sin. While born-again believers may strive for Christ-likeness, he cannot attain perfection. Once a sinner turned to Christ, he becomes a new creature. He is set apart or sanctified by God to start a new life, stop doing sins, and avoid or prevent evil in his life. Sanctification starts to operate at his conversion going through life until he is finally raptured to God.

Hacking Agag to Pieces

Born again believers are saved from sin but they are not saved to sin. Christians are not exempted from sin despite of being saved from it. In fact nothing hinders them to commit sin if they want to. What is the reason why becoming a born again believer does not exempt him from sin?

While it is true the fortress of sin has been broken at conversion the tendency or inclination to commit sin still exists. It is not completely deleted or erased at once by turning to Christ. It takes a process known as *mortification*, to absolutely obliterate the inclination of sin in every human heart. Mortification, like sanctification, does not completely operate not until the believer is glorified.

For Christians to stop sinning is to put to death the activities or vices of the heart that do sin. Just like Agag who was spared from the sword by King Saul should be ruthlessly be hacked to pieces. There should not be any semblance of sin left in the heart. Every sin should be entirely destroyed without mercy. For one who became a Christian but refuses to kill entirely some of his secret or pet sins he cannot stop sinning. These sins will trigger him to destruction.

To completely eradicate sin in one's heart is not an easy task. A constant mortification of sin should be done until the believer is in glory. Mortification does not involve self-flagellation or self-sacrifice, torture to the body, or deprive the body of its basic needs. Mortification is one that is active as led by the Holy Spirit of God in the believer's heart. It includes putting to death the faculties, properties, wisdom, craft, subtlety, and strength of the flesh. All powers, strength, vigor, life, and effects that produce sin should be taken away by the Holy Spirit.

To mortify oneself is not a mysterious activity. It does not involve divination or requires signs or extra-terrestrial forces for mortification to happen. It is just as simple as to obey the Scriptures. The following statements outline how to mortify the tendency to sin in the life of the believer. *One*, abstain from fleshly lusts. This is simply staying away or stop lusting. To quit doing lust is mortification. *Two*, make no provision for the flesh. This is simply refusal to accommodate fleshly lusts. If one is tempted with sexual urge, stop entertaining those mental images of lust. *Three*, fix one's heart in Christ. This is simply making Christ the focus of the believer's heart. If the heart worships only

Christ he becomes Christ-like. *Four*, meditate on God's Word. Success in life for believers is determined on the meditation of God's Word every day. God's Word hacks to pieces fleshly desires. *Five*, pray without ceasing. Prayer is power. Continuous prayer before God adds strength against sin. *Six*, watch and pray. The most effective prayer for mortifying sin includes confession and repentance of sin. *Seven*, exercise self-control. Every believer must exercise self-discipline of his heart. It is a watchful discipline that refuses to pander to the appetites of the body at the soul's expense. And *eight*, be filled with the Holy Spirit. Just as alcohol influences mental powers of man, one who is filled with Holy Spirit is empowered to mortify sin. In fact it is the Holy Spirit of God in the believer's heart that does the work of mortification.

As mentioned, to mortify oneself is to actually hack Agag into pieces. Sin is not mortified when it is just merely covered, only internalized, exchanged for another sin, conscience has not been appeased, and merely repressed. Sin must be stricken at its head to stop it from coming back. Believers should be courageous enough to do this. Incidentally, mortification only applies to believers. Those without Christ need first salvation through faith in Christ.

Handling Temptation

Modern society views sin differently from what the Bible teaches. People are proud of when they do sin. It means that doing sin brings them happiness. Today's modern society glorifies evil hurts.

However, a genuine born-again believer cannot tolerate sin as a source of "feeling good" or happiness. The Bible bluntly teaches that even pride is sin contrary to what society reckons it.

Sin occurs when a Christian yields to temptation. Temptation itself is not sin. But before God's eyes there is no temptation but tests or trials. When the believer passes the test it is not temptation. But when he succumbs to it, such test has become a temptation.

Sin does not occur with forces beyond the believer's power to control. It is a false claim that when one is tempted and has succumbed to it as a result he sinned because he has no option not to do it. Sin does not come with demons or satanic forces with it. It comes or strikes any person with the power to repel it. For the believer, sin has been a defeated enemy. It has no power at all to control the Christian's heart if resisted. Every Christian has the power to resist over temptation. When resisted, sin flies away. It does not hurt the believer.

Temptation that leads to sin must be known to every Christian. One must know the nature, extent, and escape of temptation. Firstly, temptation comes without notice. It tries to ambush any Christian so that he will be drawn to sin. A classic example illustrates this. A new employee discovered a huge sum of money on his table. Instead of putting it to his pocket he brought it to his boss. The boss told the employee he passed the test. Now, if he kept the money instead of giving it to his boss he committed sin. Seeing that money on the table is a temptation to keep it personally. But, he resisted the temptation by bringing it to his boss. Hence, the test did not become temptation.

Secondly, temptation is human. Temptation is not supernatural. It does not come with satanic forces so that it becomes uncontrollable. The temptation one experiences is the very same temptation that was tested and passed by another faithful Christian. The temptations that modern Christians do experience are the very temptations that Christians in the past did experience. They are ordinary and simple temptations. They can be refused and resisted. They never come with overpowering forces.

Thirdly, temptation is limited to human capacity. God does not give tests or trials beyond the power the Christians can bear. A classic illustration will help this. Peter was told by Jesus that Satan has tempted him to do anything to protect Christ from going to the Cross. But Christ told Peter that he could bear it since He has prayed for him. Every Christian experiences tests from God. However, at the same time God gives to him enough grace to sustain it. There is not one temptation to the believer that he is not able to resist it if he wants to.

Fourthly, temptation provides a way out. There exists always an escape for every temptation. For the believer, to endure the trial and never succumb to it is an evidence of the way out of temptation. If someone has been despised, maligned, maltreated, dishonored, treated unjustly he can escape from temptation to take revenge or angry at the attacker by accepting the bad treatment or ridicule. Instead of developing anger he must count it all joy for the sake of Christ. He will endure temptation by meditating on God's Word, praying that test should not be turned into temptation, and resisting Satan and yielding to God completely.

Keeping a Pure Mind

Sins can be committed physically and mentally. There exists greater destructive power to the conscience of the sins that are committed in the mind. It is more dangerous than sins committed physically. **Thought** sins can hardly be removed from human conscience. When sins are engraved in the mind it is very difficult to undo. Every believer should be warned that thought sins are more dangerous than sins committed physically.

There exists a danger to a sinful thought life. Thought sins directly involve the soul and work to bias towards evil. When sin is incubated in thought it ripens into action. Once it acts it becomes a habit or character. When sin becomes a character it reaps a destiny. So, all sins lay their groundwork in the mind.

Mind and heart are biblically synonymous. The Bible teaches that evil things originate from the heart. This means that sins that are actually committed have been incubated in the human heart. The inner faculties – mind, emotions, desire, memory, and imagination all are responsible for thought sins that directly affect the soul. Christ emphasized this danger of thought sins against the Pharisees. The Pharisees were more concerned of the external character than the internal activities of the heart.

The heart must be carefully guarded. It is easier to put an end of sins that are done physically. But thought sins are hard to eradicate since they leave indelible sinful marks in the human conscience. Once sin starts in the heart it is difficult to mortify and destroy. Christians should guard this particular area before it is too late.

How does the mind sin? There are three major ways where the mind does commit sin. *Firstly*, sins of remembering. This is to cherish the past memories. Since sin leaves indelible marks in the heart it is easy to remember those sins that Christians had committed before they got saved. These sinful garbage of memories have the tendency to linger and stalk around the mind, and hence, even a faint signal to recall of its images will court a serious disaster. The only solution to this is to put an end or refuse abruptly to entertain these garbage.

Secondly, sins of scheming. This is plotting to commit sins in the future. This is similar to commit the crime of murder. Premeditation is an essential requisite of the crime of murder. Premeditation is planning in advance the techniques, methods, tools, or resources to be used to harm someone. Hence, biblically speaking, murder has been already committed in the mind of the criminal.

Thirdly, sins of imagining. This is another unique of committing sin in the mind. This is done by drawing up mental images of sin. Evil people love to daydream to gain immediate wealth by robbery, raping a woman, or kill a person. This sin is more imaginary than actual. This is more dangerous because this is not clearly detected by human beings or even technology.

How can these thought sins be avoided or prevented? The following are practical ways to counter thought sins. *One*, confess and forsake sin. God is ready to forgive if one confesses and forsakes his sin before God. *Two*, refuse to entertain those garbage-thoughts. *Three*, feed on the Word of God. When the mind is filled with God's Word, it has no room to entertain garbage. *Four*, avoid evil attractions. Anything that provokes thoughts to sin should be avoided. Exposure to garbage images or activities reactivates thought sins. And *five*, cultivate the love of God. To cultivate God's love is to obey Him faithfully regardless of circumstances.

Holding to the Mystery of Faith with a Clear Conscience

This last chapter illustrates the severity of sin as taught in the Bible. The Puritan writer Jeremiah Burroughs suggests that the smallest sin is more evil than the greatest affliction. Sin condemns one to hell. Affliction does not condemn any sinner.

However, modern society has redefined sin as shame. As a result a sinner does not feel good about himself due to his sin but because of shame before the public eye. The self-esteem philosophy has made sin taken lightly that modernists see shame as more worse than sin which causes it.

To illustrate this point, a professor tells of his mother dying in bed claiming, "I'm so glad that the Lord forgives me all of my sins; I've been a great sinner, you know." The professor rejects his mother's claim that she is a great sinner. She is just suffering from unhealthy "shame". This is the result of self-esteem psychology. It reduces sin at its face value. It redefines sin as "shame' to make it palatable to human feeling. Sin is discouraging, but admission of guilt shows defeat. He further suggests that people are not so bad that they deserve Hell. They rather deserve grace than Hell and people are worthy of it.

This allegation attacks, the very root why sinner requires underserved grace to save him from sin. God saves any repentant sinner who comes to him not because he is worthy or he deserves it. Christ saves sinners because of God's unmerited favor and mercy. There is nothing in the sinner that would indicate the ground for salvation. In fact, the sinner deserves hell than Heaven.

Psychology absolves any sins of any individuals. To make it authoritative psychologists try to use Scriptures to support their claim of healing from sin. Sin is watered down in psychology. There is no such thing as sin but only shame that exists in the world.

The church has not been spared from the self-esteem philosophy of sin. When a sinner worries about sin. The church will just tell him not to worry about it but to accept Christ. When along the way sin beats him, he is advised to look on Christ and not settle it down first.

No matter what word is used to color sin to make it appear more beautiful it does not change its sting. The church and each individual is responsible before God for their own sin. They should settle it down before its terrible price comes.

The following is a list of practical principles in order to recover a healthy conscience. *One*, do not underestimate the seriousness of sin. Sin destroys man's relationship to God. *Two*, the heart must determine purposely not to sin. A determination to fight against sin at all cost is the basis of holy living. *Three*, being suspicious of individuals' spirituality. This is to always check the status of one's life and take precautionary measures against sin. *Four*, resistance of the first hint of evil desire. The best antidote for sin is direct refusal of sin at the time of its conception and not at its execution. Avoidance of lust is effective when blunt refusal is executed at its first suggestion. *Five*, meditation on the Word of God. God's Word is the most powerful weapon against it. It fills the heart, controls the mind, and direct man's step. *Six*, instant repentance over lapses. Sin must be named and confessed before God. *Seven*, continually watch and pray. God's protection is the best security against sin. This can be done through constant prayers. And *eight*, being involved in the church, believers strengthen one another. Each Christian must be involved in church activities or programs for the advancement of the gospel of Christ.

APPENDICES

Are You Saved?

Absolutely Free

In this day and time, it's not often that someone offers an absolutely free gift. Yet here is the most wonderful and precious free gift especially for you! It has already been paid for by someone else. Please read on to find out more.

This gift is *ETERNAL LIFE* in a glorious **Heaven**.

It is difficult for men to accept the thought of this being a free gift. Man wants to earn everlasting life.

The Holy Bible says: "For by grace are ye saved through faith; and that not of yourselves: it is the gift of God: Not of works, lest any man should boast." (Ephesians 2:8-9) The Bible says: "…the gift of God is eternal life through Jesus Christ our Lord." (Romans 6:23)

A gift is not something we earn or work for. We receive gifts out of love. In fact, "GRACE" means: "Unmerited, or unearned favour." If we work for something, it is not a gift, but a wage.

The only wages we receive from God is Hell! "For the wages of sin is death…" (Romans 6:23a) "…and sin, **We earn death in hell, but God gives us Heaven through Jesus** when it is finished, bringeth forth death" (James 1:15b). "In flaming fire taking vengeance on them that know not God, and that obey not the gospel of our Lord Jesus Christ." (2 Thessalonians 1:8)

The Lord Jesus Christ paid for this gift with His own dear shed blood on the cross. "…without shedding of blood is no remission." (Hebrews 9:22b) "…the blood of Jesus Christ his Son cleanseth us from all sin." (1 John 1:7b) "But God commendeth his love toward us, in that, while we were yet sinners, Christ died for us." (Romans 5:8)

Receive this absolutely free gift TODAY! Come to God in humble prayer, admit your guilt as a sinner before a Holy God, turn to God from your sin by faith (repent), asking God to save you through the Lord Jesus Christ. "But as many as received him, to them gave he power to become the sons of God, even to them that believe on his name." (John 1:12)

"Testifying both to the Jews, and also to the Greeks, repentance toward God, and faith toward our Lord Jesus Christ." (Acts 20:21) "For whosoever (YOU!!) shall call upon the name of the Lord shall be saved." (Romans 10:13 "   …behold, now is the accepted time, behold, now is the day of salvation." (2 Corinthians 6:2b)

Please let us know in writing (write your name and phone number below and bring, mail or email this tract back to us) if you have trusted Christ's promise to save you and give you eternal life.

Your Name: _______________________

Your Phone: _______________________

METROPOLITAN BIBLE BAPTIST CHURCH
11-13 Royal Street, Kenwick WA 6107
(Entrance on Royal Street)
Phone: (08) 9459 1233
Website: www.mbbc.com.au
Email: pastor@mbbc.com.au

<u>CHURCH SERVICE TIMES</u>:
Sunday Doctrine Class — 9:30 a.m.
Sunday Worship Service — 10:40 a.m.
Sunday Evening Service — 5:00 p.m.
Wednesday Evening Service — 7:00 p.m.

Dr Romeo Macale, Pastor

www.ingramcontent.com/pod-product-compliance
Lightning Source LLC
Chambersburg PA
CBHW031109250726

48655CB00004B/1646